Benchmark and Unit Tests

Grade 2

Houghton Mifflin Harcourt™

Contents

Grade 2 Benchmark and Unit Tests

Reading and Analyzing Text

**Read the story "Autumn Treasures" before answering
Numbers 1 through 5.**

Autumn Treasures

by Edna Ledgard

illustrated by Helen Cogancherry

Grace found a pretty red leaf. She found a big orange leaf and three yellow leaves. She even found a green leaf. She tucked them into her pocket and ran to school.

Her friends had leaves, too. Red leaves. Yellow leaves. Orange leaves. Some children had brought acorns and horse chestnuts, too.

"I'm going to keep my leaves forever," Grace told Miss Hill.

Miss Hill smiled. She passed out cans of old peeled crayons and sheets of white paper. Grace put a leaf on her desk, bumpy side up under the paper. Carefully she rubbed the side of her red crayon against the paper. It made a leaf pattern.

Soon Grace had a red leaf, an orange leaf, and three yellow leaves on her paper.

Grace took her black crayon and colored hard in all the empty spaces.

Miss Hill pinned the beautiful leaf patterns all around the room. She put the real leaves on a shelf with some acorns and horse chestnuts.

In a few days, the real leaves had turned dry and brown, but the leaf patterns were still bright.

"What a good way to keep my leaves forever!" said Grace.

Now answer Numbers 1 through 5. Base your answers on the story "Autumn Treasures."

1 Where does this story MOSTLY take place?

Ⓐ in a forest

Ⓑ at the park

Ⓒ at Grace's house

Ⓓ in Grace's classroom

2 What does Grace do FIRST when she finds her leaves?

Ⓕ makes leaf patterns

Ⓖ tucks them in her pocket

Ⓗ takes them to her teacher

Ⓘ hangs them on the wall at school

3 Why does Grace put the leaf "bumpy side up" under the paper?

Ⓐ to rub a leaf pattern

Ⓑ to help the leaf dry faster

Ⓒ to help the leaf last longer

Ⓓ to make the leaf turn brown

4 Read this sentence from the story.

Miss Hill pinned the beautiful leaf patterns all around the room.

What does the word *pinned* mean in the sentence above?

(F) covered

(G) dried

(H) held

(I) hung

5 What happens at the end of the story?

(A) The leaves start to fall.

(B) The real leaves turn brown.

(C) Grace makes leaf patterns.

(D) Grace finds a pretty red leaf.

Name _____ Date _____

Read the article "The World of Bats" before answering Numbers 6 through 10.

The World of Bats

If an animal flies, is it a bird? Not necessarily. Bats, like birds, have wings and can fly. However, bats and birds are really very different. There are about 1,000 types of bats that can be found all over the world. Most bats, though, share some common traits.

What does a bat look like?

Bats have a body that resembles a mouse. Their hands and arms are covered by a thin layer of skin. This allows their hands and arms to work like wings. Some bats have long tails, while others do not have any tail at all. Most bats have hair that helps to keep them warm.

Some bats are extremely large. They can be more than five feet long from the tip of one wing to the tip of the other wing. Some bats are very small, sometimes less than two inches from one wing tip to the other.

Bats have two eyes and can see very well. Some bats have large eyes, while others have very small eyes.

Bats also have two ears. They can move their ears to listen to sounds. They hear sounds very well, but they also use their hearing in other ways. They can use their hearing so they do not bump into things, and they can even use it to find their food.

Just like people, bats have two sets of teeth in their lifetime. They have baby teeth when they are young. As they grow up, they lose their baby teeth and grow a new set of adult teeth.

How do bats live?

Bats can see well even when it's dark, which means they can hunt for food at night. Bats eat a variety of things. Many bats eat bugs, while other bats eat fruit.

Because they search for food at night, bats usually sleep during the day. Some often sleep in caves, barns, or holes in trees. Others sleep in houses that people build for them. When a bat sleeps, it hangs upside down from its feet.

How do bats help people?

Bats help people in several ways. For example, some bats eat the bugs that bite people and destroy plants. Bats can also help people by eating fruit. After they eat the fruit, bats sometimes drop seeds. The seeds then grow into new plants.

Bats are very interesting and unusual animals. Not only can they fly, but they also make the world a more pleasant place for people.

6

Name _____ Date _____

Now answer Numbers 6 through 10. Base your answers on the article "The World of Bats."

6 Which of the following BEST tells how the author feels about bats?

- (F) Some bats eat bugs.
- (G) Some bats sleep in houses.
- (H) They are very much like birds.
- (I) They are helpful and interesting animals.

7 Which of these words from the story comes FIRST in ABC order?

- (A) tail
- (B) ears
- (C) wings
- (D) mouse

8 Which of the following is true about ALL bats?

- (F) They have two ears.
- (G) They are very large.
- (H) They have long tails.
- (I) They have small eyes.

9 How are bats and people ALIKE?

Ⓐ Both have long tails.

Ⓑ Both have small eyes.

Ⓒ Both usually sleep during the day.

Ⓓ Both have two sets of teeth in their lifetime.

10 How does the picture help you understand the article?

Ⓕ It shows how bats can help people.

Ⓖ It shows how bats use their hearing.

Ⓗ It shows how bats and birds are alike.

Ⓘ It shows how bats hang upside down to sleep.

Read the story "That Cat!" before answering Numbers 11 through 15.

That Cat!

by Susan Campbell Bartoletti

illustrated by David LaFleur

Dad poked his hand into my basket. "What's that?" he asked.

"Mew," said the basket.

Dad yanked his hand away. "Oh no," he said. "Not a cat. No way."

I pulled Checkers from the basket. "It's not a cat. It's a kitten. Can I keep him? Please?"

Checkers wasn't any trouble at all—until he grew into a cat.

Dad frowned for a minute, thinking. Then he rubbed Checkers under the chin. "You'll have to take good care of him."

I hugged Checkers. "I will," I promised. "He won't be any trouble at all."

And Checkers wasn't—until he grew into a cat.

He wanted to be the first one *in* the house—and the first one *out* of the house. Sometimes, he tripped Dad.

"That cat!" Dad complained.

Checkers climbed onto our roof. He had no trouble getting down. Usually he aimed for Dad.

"That cat!" Dad hollered.

Checkers flushed the toilet and watched the water circle away.

"That cat!" Dad groaned.

Checkers hid in strange places. He liked to surprise people.

One day he hid under the couch. Dad walked by with a glass of orange juice.

Checkers jumped out. He curled around Dad's ankle and attacked Dad's toes. Orange juice sloshed all over the floor.

Dad hollered and put Checkers outside. "Scram, cat," he said. And he slammed the door.

Dad washed the scratches and peeled open a bandage. He wrapped it around his big toe. He opened four more for his ankle.

I watched from the window. Checkers looked insulted as he walked down the road.

"I'm sorry Checkers scratched you," I said. "He was just playing. He didn't mean to hurt you."

"Don't worry," said Dad. "That cat will be back."

After supper I called for Checkers. But Checkers didn't come.

Nighttime came. I called and called. I banged his food dish with a spoon. But still no Checkers.

I left the porch light on. But the next morning Checkers still wasn't there.

I carried a picture of Checkers to all the neighbors. I drew posters and hung them all over. But nobody found Checkers.

Days went by. Life wasn't the same without that cat.

I was angry with Dad. I didn't think he missed Checkers at all.

Then one night the phone rang. "We'll be right over," said Dad.

We drove to a nearby farm. The farmer opened the barn door. Out ran a black-and-white cat.

"Checkers!" I cried. I scooped him up. Checkers purred. We rubbed noses. "I missed you!" I said.

The farmer smiled. "Good thing I saw that ad in the paper."

I looked at Dad. "You put an ad in the paper?"

Dad's face turned red. He nodded.

He petted Checkers. Checkers batted at him with his paw.

Dad laughed. "That cat," he said. "It's good to have him back."

Now answer Numbers 11 through 15. Base your answers on the story "That Cat!"

⓫ Why does Checkers run away?

   ⓐ   Checkers wants to surprise Dad.

   ⓑ   Checkers wants to live on a farm.

   ⓒ   Dad spills orange juice on Checkers.

   ⓓ   Dad yells at Checkers and puts him outside.

⓬ Read the glossary entry below.

> **peel**, *verb* **1.** to strip or take paint from a wall. **2.** to pull or separate objects. **3.** to take the rind off of an orange. **4.** to move a ball in the game of croquet.

Read this sentence from the story.

   Dad washed the scratches and peeled open a bandage.

Which meaning BEST fits the way the word *peeled* is used in the sentence above?

   ⓕ   meaning 1

   ⓖ   meaning 2

   ⓗ   meaning 3

   ⓘ   meaning 4

Name _____ Date _____

13 How does Dad help find Checkers?

(A) He puts up posters.

(B) He calls the neighbors.

(C) He puts an ad in the paper.

(D) He leaves on the porch light.

14 How does Dad feel at the end of the story?

(F) He is happy that they found Checkers.

(G) He is sad because they cannot find Checkers.

(H) He is upset and gives Checkers to the farmer.

(I) He is angry and wishes Checkers would run away again.

15 What can you tell about Dad from this story?

(A) He is very clumsy.

(B) He likes dogs more than cats.

(C) He really wanted to find Checkers.

(D) He does not want Checkers anymore.

13

Read the article "Poison Ivy" before answering Numbers 16 through 20.

Poison Ivy

Have you ever touched poison ivy? If you have, you most likely know that it can make you itch. Poison ivy is a plant that produces oil that can cause you to get a rash if you touch it or bump into it. The rash may have red bumps and blisters. It will be very itchy. It can last for several weeks.

It is important to know what poison ivy looks like so that you can stay away from it. It is a green plant that has leaves in groups of three. It can grow as a vine or a bush. It might be growing in the woods or in your backyard.

What should you do if you see that you have touched poison ivy? Tell a grownup. Then quickly go wash any part of your skin that has touched the plant. You need to use soap and water to get the plant's oil off your skin. If you do not, you will probably start getting a rash in about ten minutes.

There is a rhyme about poison ivy. Leaves of three—let them be! This is good to remember.

Now answer Numbers 16 through 20. Base your answers on the article "Poison Ivy."

16 Why did the author MOST LIKELY write this article?

(F) to tell readers about different rashes

(G) to give readers facts about poison ivy

(H) to tell readers how to grow poison ivy

(I) to teach readers about interesting bushes

17 Read this sentence from the article.

It can last for several weeks.

What does the word *last* mean in the sentence above?

(A) continue

(B) end

(C) finally

(D) late

18 How is poison ivy DIFFERENT from other plants?

(F) It has red leaves.

(G) It only has one leaf.

(H) It has leaves in groups of three.

(I) It is a plant that does not have leaves.

Name _____ Date _____

19 Read this sentence from the article.

> **What should you do if you see that you**
>
> **have touched poison ivy?**

What does the word *touched* mean in the sentence above?

Ⓐ felt

Ⓑ saw

Ⓒ stopped

Ⓓ washed

20 How does the picture help you understand the article?

Ⓕ It shows what to do if you touch poison ivy.

Ⓖ It shows how long it takes for a rash to form.

Ⓗ It shows what poison ivy looks like up close.

Ⓘ It shows what a poison ivy rash can look like.

Name _____ Date _____

Phonics

Answer Numbers 21 through 30. Choose the best answer for each question.

21 Which word has the SAME vowel sound as the word *wake* in the sentence below?

It was still dark when my brother told me to wake up.

(A) save

(B) splash

(C) tack

(D) wash

22 Which word has the SAME vowel sound as the word *spoke* in the sentence below?

He spoke quietly so Mom wouldn't hear him.

(F) moth

(G) note

(H) sock

(I) spot

Name _____ Date _____

23 Which word is CORRECT and BEST completes the
sentence below?

We got _____ and tiptoed out of the house.

- (A) dessed
- (B) dress
- (C) dressed
- (D) ressed

24 Which word has the SAME vowel sound as the word *plan* in the
sentence below?

Our plan was to give Mom a new garden for her birthday.

- (F) dad
- (G) late
- (H) plane
- (I) plum

25 Which word has the SAME vowel sound as the word *shed* in the
sentence below?

We got the plants we had hidden in the shed.

- (A) dish
- (B) mess
- (C) sale
- (D) shade

Name _____ Date _____

26 Which word has the SAME sound as the underlined part of the word *began* in the sentence below?

Next we began digging holes for the plants.

- (F) bridge
- (G) cage
- (H) gate
- (I) gem

27 Which word has the SAME vowel sound as the word *pots* in the sentence below?

We took the plants out of their pots and put one in each hole.

- (A) drop
- (B) note
- (C) plate
- (D) pole

28 Which word has the SAME vowel sound as the word *gift* in the sentence below?

We watered the garden and then let Mom see our gift.

- (F) I
- (G) gave
- (H) smile
- (I) will

29 Which word has the SAME sound as the underlined part of the word *face* in the sentence below?

We could tell by the look on her fa<u>c</u>e that she was surprised.

- Ⓐ act
- Ⓑ cake
- Ⓒ sand
- Ⓓ tack

30 Which word is CORRECT and BEST completes the sentence below?

Mom liked her garden! She picked a red flower with white _____.

- Ⓕ sips
- Ⓖ steps
- Ⓗ stripes
- Ⓘ trips

Revising and Editing

Read the introduction and the story "Sam the Skunk" before answering Numbers 1 through 5.

Perla wrote this story about a skunk. Read her story and think about the changes she should make.

Sam the Skunk

(1) Sam the skunk lived in a hole by a big trees. (2) He wanted to be friends with the other animals. (3) He waved at them and gav them a smile. (4) Each time he tried to move closer, the animals ran away. (5) They were afraid of Sam's smell. (6) No one wanted to be his friend.

(7) One day Sam. (8) He heard a pretty song. (9) It was Bluebird sitting in the top of his tree! (10) After she finished singing, Sam thanked her for the nice song. (11) Bluebird smiled. (12) She said she wanted to live in his tree. (13) Then she could sing for him every day.

(14) Sam asked Bluebird why his smell did not scare her. (15) Bluebird laughed. (16) She said that his smell could not reach her. (17) Way up in the treetop. (18) Sam clapped and did a little dance? (19) At last, Sam had a friend!

Name _____ Date _____

Now answer Numbers 1 through 5. Base your answers on the changes Perla should make.

1 Look at sentence 1 again.

> **(1) Sam the skunk lived in a hole by a big trees.**

How should this sentence be changed?

- Ⓐ change *Sam* to **sam**
- Ⓑ change *trees* to **tree**
- Ⓒ change the period (**.**) to a question mark (**?**)

2 Look at sentence 3 again.

> **(3) He waved at them and gav them a smile.**

How should this sentence be changed?

- Ⓕ change *He* to **His**
- Ⓖ change *gav* to **gave**
- Ⓗ change *smile* to **smiles**

3 Look at these sentences again.

(7) One day Sam.

(8) He heard a pretty song.

(11) Bluebird smiled.

Which sentence is NOT a complete sentence?

Ⓐ sentence 7

Ⓑ sentence 8

Ⓒ sentence 11

4 Look at sentence 18 again.

(18) Sam clapped and did a little dance?

How should this sentence be changed?

Ⓕ change *little* to **Little**

Ⓖ change *dance* to **dances**

Ⓗ change the question mark (**?**) to a period (**.**)

5 Look at these sentences again.

(15) Bluebird laughed.

(17) Way up in the treetop.

(19) At last, Sam had a friend!

Which sentence is NOT a complete sentence?

Ⓐ sentence 15

Ⓑ sentence 17

Ⓒ sentence 19

Read the introduction and the story "A Great Kite" before answering Numbers 6 through 10.

Darius wrote this story about his new kite. Read his story and think about the changes he should make.

A Great Kite

(1) Do you like kites (2) If you do, you will love my octopus kite! (3) It has a round head with big eyes. (4) It also has eight leg just like a real octopus. (5) My kite looks great when it flies!

(6) To fly the kite, I hold onto the string and run. (7) At first, the octopus looks flat, and it stays closs to the ground. (8) Then the wind lifts it into the air. (9) As it goes up, the head fills with air.

(10) First, I pull the string tight. (11) Then, little by little, the kite goes higher. (12) My octopus kite is high up in the sky. (13) The wind makes its legs move. (14) It looks like the octopus is alive. (15) It is the best kites I have ever had!

Now answer Numbers 6 through 10. Base your answers on the changes Darius should make.

6 Look at sentence 1 again.

(1) Do you like kites

How should this sentence be changed?

F change *you* to **You**

G change *kites* to **kite**

H put a question mark (**?**) at the end of the sentence

7 Look at sentence 4 again.

(4) It also has eight leg just like a real octopus.

How should this sentence be changed?

A change *It* to **it**

B change *leg* to **legs**

C change the period (**.**) to a question mark (**?**)

8 Look at sentence 7 again.

(7) At first, the octopus looks flat, and it stays closs to the ground.

How should this sentence be changed?

F change *first* to **last**

G change *closs* to **close**

H change the period (**.**) to a question mark (**?**)

Name _____ Date _____

9 Look at these sentences again.

(10) First, I pull the string tight.

(11) Then, little by little, the kite goes higher.

(12) My octopus kite is high up in the sky.

Which word should be added at the beginning of sentence 12?

Ⓐ Finally,

Ⓑ Before,

Ⓒ Tomorrow,

10 Look at sentence 15 again.

(15) It is the best kites I have ever had!

How should this sentence be changed?

Ⓕ change *It* to **Its**

Ⓖ change *kites* to **kite**

Ⓗ change *I* to **me**

Writing to Narrate

Read the prompt and plan your response.

Most people have done something that made them feel proud.

Think about a time you did something that made you feel proud.

Now write a story about the time you did something that made you feel proud.

Use this space to make your notes before you begin writing. The writing on this page will NOT be scored.

_____

_____

_____

_____

_____

_____

Name _____ Date _____

Begin writing your response here. The writing on this page and the next page WILL be scored.

_____

_____

_____

_____

_____

_____

_____

_____

_____

_____

Name _____ Date _____

_____

_____

_____

_____

_____

_____

_____

_____

_____

_____

_____

Reading Complex Text

Read the story "Camping with Cousins." As you read, stop and answer each question. Use evidence from the story to support your answers.

Camping with Cousins

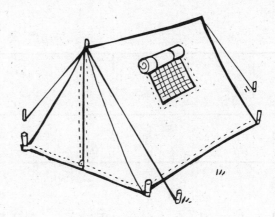

Our cousin Frank was coming over to spend the night. My older brother Jacob and I had a very difficult job to do. We had to teach Frank all about backyard camping. "Mom, you know he will ruin the whole night. He won't stay outside. Can't he just stay in?"

"Now Lucy, Frank doesn't know what he is missing," said Mom. "You have to show him how much fun backyard camping can be."

My cousin Frank doesn't like the outdoors. Frank thinks that going outside is no fun. He'd rather stay inside and read books or play video games. He says that's where the big adventures are.

I only stay inside to practice the piano. Otherwise, I'm out the door. I tell Frank that going outdoors is more fun and exciting than staying indoors, but he never listens. Well, this time he just might.

1 Why is an outdoor setting important to this story?

_____

_____

_____

Mom, Jacob, and I put up the tent, but Frank would only sit on the back porch. It was a start. Frank looked around and said, "This is as far as I'm going. There are too many bugs out here."

Mom, Jacob, and I roasted marshmallows over the fire. Our dog Duke stayed with us. Duke drooled a lot from the sweet smell. He was a wet mess.

Frank said he wanted to roast marshmallows, too. He moved to the fire. After a while, he was smiling. He had figured out exactly how long to toast each marshmallow to perfection.

Now seemed like the best time to get Frank to stay outside. "Hey Frank, I don't think the bugs are too bad tonight," I said. "What about giving the tent a try?"

Name _____ Date _____

2 Why does Lucy think Frank might stay outside?

_____

_____

_____

_____

Frank looked back at the house and said, "Maybe I could give backyard camping a try. The marshmallows are pretty good after all." I couldn't believe it. He wanted to stay outside with us!

Mom made sure the tent had plenty of blankets, pillows, and flashlights. We didn't want to take any chances with Frank.

Soon after everyone got cozy, the gentle breeze outside became a strong wind. Next, we heard sprinkling against the tent. Then, suddenly, the clouds burst open and the rain came pouring down. The wind screamed. I was scared. My brother hid under the blankets. Duke whined. What were we going to do? Our whole night of camping was ruined.

When I looked at Frank, he had a big smile on his face. "Frank, how could you be happy at a time like this?" I asked. Frank just smiled and said, "I've never been outside in a rainstorm before. This is like a big adventure."

3 Frank says, "This is like a big adventure." Why is this surprising?

_____

_____

_____

Frank was right. This was a big adventure. The storm wasn't a dangerous one. It just sounded scary. Pretty soon my brother came out from under the blankets, and Duke stopped whining. We all started to pretend we were on a ship that was lost at sea. Now this was the most fun I ever had camping. Good thing Frank was here.

4 Retell what happens FIRST, NEXT, and LAST in this story.

_____

_____

_____

_____

_____

Name _____ Date _____

Reading and Analyzing Text

**Read the story "A New Life for Tweet" before answering
Numbers 1 through 10.**

A New Life for Tweet

Tweet was a quiet little bird. All day long, he sat alone in his
tree. He never sang. He just watched the world around him. Tweet
watched frogs and turtles swimming in the pond. He watched
rabbits and squirrels playing in the woods. Day after day, he sat
on the same branch and watched the same things.

Then one day, there was something new to see. It happened
right in Tweet's tree. Four little eggs in a nearby nest began to
hatch. Tap, tap, tap. The baby birds used their beaks to crack their
shells. As soon as the birds hatched, they opened their mouths
wide. They were hungry! Tweet watched Mother Bird fly off to
find food for them.

One of the babies kept trying to find its mother. It wiggled
away from the other birds. Tweet got worried. The baby was very
close to the edge of the nest.

All at once, the baby bird fell! Tweet felt unsure about leaving
his branch, but time was running out. He flew toward the little bird
with his heart pounding. Would he reach it in time?

Tweet flew as fast as he could. He swooped below the baby
bird. It landed on Tweet's soft back! Then up, up, up Tweet flew.
He put the little bird back in its nest.

Just then, Mother Bird came back with some tasty bugs for the hungry little birds. She thanked Tweet for helping her baby. To repay his kindness, she gave him the biggest, fattest bug. Tweet smiled and stood up tall. He was glad he had left his branch.

After that, Tweet always sat near the nest. When Mother Bird left to find food, she did not worry. Tweet's pretty song filled the forest. It let her know that her babies were safe in their nest!

36

Name _____ Date _____

Now answer Numbers 1 through 10. Base your answers on the story "A New Life for Tweet."

1 At the beginning of the story, what does Tweet do?

Ⓐ He plays in the woods.

Ⓑ He just sits alone in his tree.

Ⓒ He swims with the frogs and turtles.

Ⓓ He rescues a bird.

2 Read this sentence from the story.

Tweet watched frogs and turtles swimming in the pond.

What does the word *pond* mean in the sentence above?

Ⓕ a wide river

Ⓖ a small lake

Ⓗ a little creek

Ⓘ a sandy beach

Name _____ Date _____

3 Read this sentence from the story.

Then one day, there was something new to see.

What does the word *see* mean in the sentence above?

- Ⓐ ocean
- Ⓑ look at
- Ⓒ hide from
- Ⓓ learn from

4 Read this sentence from the story.

The baby birds used their beaks to crack their shells.

What does the word *beaks* mean in the sentence above?

- Ⓕ long, sharp claws
- Ⓖ loud, hungry calls
- Ⓗ short, strong wings
- Ⓘ hard, pointed mouths

5 Why does Tweet get worried?

- Ⓐ The eggs in the nest might break.
- Ⓑ A baby bird might fall out of the nest.
- Ⓒ Squirrels might get one of the baby birds.
- Ⓓ Mother Bird might not bring back any food.

Name _____ Date _____

6 Read this sentence from the story.

**Tweet felt unsure about leaving his branch,
but time was running out.**

What does the word *unsure* mean in the sentence above?

(F) not sure

(G) very sure

(H) sure again

(I) sure enough

7 Read this sentence from the story.

He flew toward the little bird with his heart pounding.

What does the word *pounding* mean in the sentence above?

(A) feeling good

(B) beating hard

(C) standing still

(D) watching closely

8 How does Tweet feel when Mother Bird thanks him?

(F) proud

(G) sad

(H) tired

(I) worried

Name _____ Date _____

9 At the end of the story, why does Tweet sing?

Ⓐ to help the baby birds fall asleep

Ⓑ to tell the baby birds how happy he is

Ⓒ to warn other birds when there is danger

Ⓓ to let Mother Bird know her babies are safe

10 How does Tweet change by the end of the story?

Ⓕ He finds out that watching others is boring.

Ⓖ He learns that helping others makes him happy.

Ⓗ He understands that making friends is hard for him.

Ⓘ He decides being quiet will keep him out of trouble.

**Read the article "Storm Safety" before answering Numbers
11 through 20.**

Storm Safety

Nature's Warnings

When the sky suddenly turns dark and the wind is strong,
beware! A dangerous storm might be coming. Storms are scary.
Watch for flashes of lightning. Listen for thunder. If nature sends
these warnings, don't wait for rain. Act right away to keep safe.

Safety Steps

At the first flash of lightning, quickly get inside a building or a
car. Do not go into a shed or baseball dugout. They are not closed
like a building, so they are not safe.

Even after you are indoors, be careful. It is not smart to go near
doors and windows. They can blow in or break. A room with no
windows is the safest place to be.

Do not wash your hands during a storm. Do not use anything
that runs on electricity either. Water and electrical lines are like
roads for lightning. Even if you really want to play computer
games, don't! It is better to be bored than to risk getting hurt.
Try reading a book instead. Reading is more fun than playing
computer games.

If you can't get to somewhere safe, stay out in the open. You may feel safe under a tree, but that is not a good place to be. Lightning is pulled toward tall poles and trees. Stay down low in an open space, and cover your ears to protect them. Loud thunder can damage your hearing.

Lightning Strikes

Lightning does not strike people very often. It is not likely that you will ever see that happen. If you do, call 9-1-1. Only trained emergency workers should care for a person who has been hit by lightning.

If you follow these rules, you should stay safe during a storm.

Now answer Numbers 11 through 20. Base your answers on the article "Storm Safety."

11 Read the chart below.

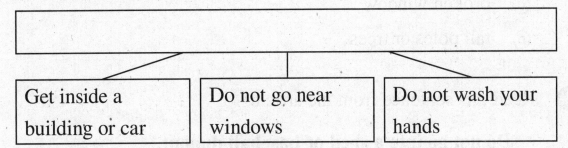

| Get inside a building or car | Do not go near windows | Do not wash your hands |

Which main idea BEST completes the chart?

Ⓐ When Storms Happen

Ⓑ What Causes Lightning

Ⓒ How to Be Safe in a Storm

Ⓓ What Emergency Workers Do

12 Read this sentence from the article.

When the sky suddenly turns dark and the wind is strong, beware!

What does the word *beware* mean in the sentence above?

Ⓕ have fun

Ⓖ stay calm

Ⓗ watch out

Ⓘ move quick

Name _____ Date _____

13 Which is a warning that a storm is coming?

Ⓐ dark sky

Ⓑ open shed

Ⓒ broken window

Ⓓ tall poles or trees

14 Read this sentence from the article.

Do not go into a shed or baseball dugout.

What does the word *baseball* mean in the sentence above?

Ⓕ a place to store things

Ⓖ base to build something on

Ⓗ a place where you start from

Ⓘ a game that is played with a ball

15 Which sentence from the article is an OPINION?

Ⓐ "Storms are scary."

Ⓑ "Do not wash your hands during a storm."

Ⓒ "Lightning does not strike people very often."

Ⓓ "Water and electrical lines are like roads for lightning."

Name _____ Date _____

16 Read this sentence from the article.

A room with no windows is the safest place to be.

What does the word *safest* mean in the sentence above?

Ⓕ not safe

Ⓖ most safe

Ⓗ more safe

Ⓘ in a safe way

17 Which sentence from the article is a FACT?

Ⓐ "It is not smart to go near doors and windows."

Ⓑ "Lightning is pulled toward tall poles and trees."

Ⓒ "It is better to be bored than to risk getting hurt."

Ⓓ "Reading is more fun than playing computer games."

18 Read this sentence from the article.

Loud thunder can damage your hearing.

What does the word *damage* mean in the sentence above?

Ⓕ carry

Ⓖ hurt

Ⓗ surprise

Ⓘ trick

45

19 Under which heading can you find what to do if someone is hurt by lightning?

Ⓐ Safety Steps

Ⓑ Storm Safety

Ⓒ Lightning Strikes

Ⓓ Nature's Warnings

20 Read this sentence from the article.

Lightning does not strike people very often.

Which word means almost the SAME as the word *strike* in the sentence above?

Ⓕ help

Ⓖ hit

Ⓗ play

Ⓘ worry

Name _____ Date _____

Phonics

Answer Numbers 21 through 30. Choose the best answer for each question.

21 Which word is CORRECT and BEST completes the
sentence below?

> **Chip the chipmunk was trying to _____ a best friend.**

- Ⓐ chance
- Ⓑ choose
- Ⓒ shoes
- Ⓓ those

22 Which form of the word *decide* is CORRECT and BEST completes
the sentence below?

> **He had a hard time _____ on just one.**

- Ⓕ deciddeing
- Ⓖ decidding
- Ⓗ decideing
- Ⓘ deciding

23 Which word is CORRECT and BEST completes the sentence below?

> **Bird's sweet _____ always made him happy.**

- Ⓐ sogn
- Ⓑ song
- Ⓒ sonj
- Ⓓ sonn

24 Which word has the SAME sound as the underlined part of the word *quick* in the sentence below?

> **He liked to play tag with Rabbit because she was so qui<u>ck</u>.**

- Ⓕ itch
- Ⓖ nice
- Ⓗ speak
- Ⓘ unit

25 Which form of the word *stuff* is CORRECT and BEST completes the sentence below?

> **Squirrel made him laugh when she _____ nuts in her cheeks.**

- Ⓐ stufed
- Ⓑ stuffd
- Ⓒ stuffed
- Ⓓ stuft

26 What does *can't* mean in the sentence below?

"I just can't make up my mind," he thought.

- Ⓕ can do
- Ⓖ can isn't
- Ⓗ cannot
- Ⓘ can't not

27 Which form of the word *smile* is CORRECT and BEST completes the sentence below?

Chip _____ as he thought about each special friend.

- Ⓐ smild
- Ⓑ smiled
- Ⓒ smileed
- Ⓓ smilled

28 Which word is CORRECT and BEST completes the sentence below?

Suddenly, Chip shouted, "I have _____ the answer!"

- Ⓕ fang
- Ⓖ foul
- Ⓗ found
- Ⓘ fount

49

Name _____ Date _____

29. What does *I'll* mean in the sentence below?

"I'll have three best friends," he said.

- Ⓐ I fall
- Ⓑ I still
- Ⓒ I will
- Ⓓ I would

30 Which word rhymes with the word *dinner* in the sentence below?

"Tonight, we will all eat dinner together!"

- Ⓕ dine
- Ⓖ diner
- Ⓗ swimmer
- Ⓘ winner

Name _____ Date _____

Revising and Editing

Read the introduction and the story "My Hiking Trips" before answering Numbers 6 through 10.

Ali wrote this story to help students stay safe while hiking. Read his story and think about the changes he should make.

My Hiking Tips

(1) I love to hike at Bastrop State Park. (2) I think you will like it, too! (3) Here are some ways to stay safe on a hike.

(4) First, plan your hike. (5) Get a map of the park. (6) Then choose the hike that is right for you.

(7) Next, pack for safety. (8) Take a first-aid kit and some water. (9) Most hikers packs a few snacks, too.

(10) Last, stay on the trails with your group. (11) That will protect you and the plants. (12) If you get off the trails, you can get bug bites or scratchs. (13) You can get stuch in the mud. (14) You can even get into poison ivy. (15) That is not fun!

(16) I hope you follow these tips. (17) If you do, you had a great hike.

Now answer Numbers 1 through 5. Base your answers on the changes Ali should make.

1 Look at these sentences again.

> **(4) First, plan your hike. (5) Get a map of the park.**
> **(6) Then choose the hike that is right for you.**

Which sentence could BEST be added after sentence 5?

- Ⓐ Be sure to wear good hiking shoes that fit you well.
- Ⓑ Use the map to find out which trails are long or steep.
- Ⓒ Taking a lot of extra things will make your pack heavy.

2 Look at sentence 9 again.

> **(9) Most hikers packs a few snacks, too.**

How should this sentence be changed?

- Ⓕ change *hikers* to **hiker**
- Ⓖ change *packs* to **pack**
- Ⓗ change *few* to **fews**

Name _____ Date _____

3 Look at sentence 10 again.

> **(10) Last, stay on the trails with your group.**

Which word is a collective noun in the sentence above?

Ⓐ trails

Ⓑ your

Ⓒ group

4 Look at sentence 13 again.

> **(13) You can get stuch in the mud.**

How should this sentence be changed?

Ⓕ change *can* to **cann**

Ⓖ change *get* to **got**

Ⓗ change *stuch* to **stuck**

5 Look at sentence 17 again.

> **(17) If you do, you had a great hike.**

How should this sentence be changed?

Ⓐ change *had* to **has**

Ⓑ change *had* to **will have**

Ⓒ change the period (**.**) to a question mark (**?**)

Read the introduction and the story "Camp Sing-Along" before answering Numbers 6 through 10.

Mei wrote this story about a music camp she went to last summer. Read her story and think about the changes she should make.

Camp Sing-Along

(1) Last summer I went to Camp Sing-Along in dallas, Texas. (2) We did a lot more than sing there. (3) We danced and put on plays, too!

(4) Our days were very busy. (5) We learnd new songs every morning. (6) Some were show tunes, and some were funny camp songs. (7) After lunch, group leaders taught us dance steps. (8) The first day, I kept tripping over my own fete. (9) My leader, Tanya ames, helped me and I got a lot better. (10) At night, we acted in skits under the stars. (11) We even put on a show for our families. (12) It was awesome!

(13) Camp showed me that it can be fun to work hard. (14) Now I sing and dance every day. (15) My friend Jane takes dance lessons after school. (16) I hope I will get to star in the Camp Sing-Along show nest summer!

Now answer Numbers 6 through 10. Base your answers on the changes Mei should make.

6 Look at sentence 1 again.

(1) Last summer I went to Camp Sing-Along in dallas, Texas.

How should this sentence be changed?

- Ⓕ change *Texas* to **texas**
- Ⓖ change *dallas* to **Dallas**
- Ⓗ change *Camp Sing-Along* to **camp sing-along**

7 Look at sentence 5 again.

(5) We learnd new songs every morning.

How should this sentence be changed?

- Ⓐ change *learnd* to **learned**
- Ⓑ change *songs* to **sons**
- Ⓒ change *every* to **everey**

8 Look at sentence 8 again.

(8) The first day, I kept tripping over my own fete.

How should this sentence be changed?

- Ⓕ change *kept* to **keeped**
- Ⓖ change *own* to **one**
- Ⓗ change *fete* to **feet**

9 Look at these sentences again.

(3) We danced and put on plays, too!

(11) We even put on a show for our families.

(15) My friend Jane takes dance lessons after school.

Which sentence does NOT belong in this story?

- Ⓐ sentence 3
- Ⓑ sentence 11
- Ⓒ sentence 15

10 Look at sentence 16 again.

(16) I hope I will get to star in the Camp
Sing-Along show nest summer!

How should this sentence be changed?

- Ⓕ change *will* to **while**
- Ⓖ change *Camp* to **Canp**
- Ⓗ change *nest* to **next**

Writing to Inform

Read the prompt and plan your response.

Most people have a game they like to play.

Think about a game you like to play.

Now write instructions that tell someone how to play that game.

Use this space to make your notes before you begin writing. The writing on this page will NOT be scored.

_____

_____

_____

_____

_____

_____

Begin writing your response here. The writing on this page and the next page WILL be scored.

_____

_____

_____

_____

_____

_____

_____

_____

_____

_____

Name _____ Date _____

_____

_____

_____

_____

_____

_____

_____

_____

_____

_____

Name _____ Date _____

Reading Complex Text

Read the article "Wondering About the Weather." As you read, stop and answer each question. Use evidence from the article to support your answers.

Wondering About the Weather

Weather is a part of every day. Some days it can be calm and peaceful. Other days it can be dark and strong. Here are some common words we use to describe the weather.

---

❶ What will this article be about?

_____

_____

_____

Clouds are made from little drops of water. Dark clouds can mean that rain is on the way. Fluffy white clouds could mean a nice day.

Rain happens when drops of water fall from the sky. Raindrops plop in ponds and make puddles on the street. When added to dirt, raindrops can make mud at your feet.

2 Why does the author use photos in this article?

_____

_____

_____

Snow is made of little pieces of ice. When it's cold, tiny snowflakes fall from the sky. If it snows for a long time, you might plan for a sled ride.

Name _____ Date _____

Sunshine gives off heat and light. It warms the air and dries the land. If you touch a window on a sunny day, the glass might feel warm on your hand.

3 Explain what might cause a window to feel warm on a sunny day.

_____

_____

_____

Temperature lets us know how cold or warm the air is. We can tell if it's time to wear a winter jacket or if it's just fine to wear a pair of shorts.

Name _____ Date _____

Wind is moving air. It can be soft like a breeze or strong like a sneeze. Soft or strong, wind can make sound. Listen and hear its song.

There are many ways to learn about weather. You can watch the news to plan for your day. You can also step outside to see what the sky looks like. Whatever the weather, be ready for how it can change your day!

---

4 Tell one way you can learn about weather. Then explain WHY the author thinks it is a good idea to learn about weather.

_____

_____

_____

_____

_____

Name _____ Date _____

Reading and Analyzing Text

**Read the story "Missing Mark" before answering
Numbers 1 through 5.**

Missing Mark

by Mary Penn
illustrated by Amy Wummer

"Who will take me to get ice cream when you're gone?"
Ashley asked. She watched her big brother, Mark, lay a shirt in his
suitcase.

"Maybe Mom. She likes ice cream," Mark said.

"Who will read me stories?"

"Maybe Grandma. She's the best story reader in the world."
Mark closed his suitcase.

"Who will draw me pictures?"

"Maybe Dad. He used to draw
pictures for me," Mark said, giving
Ashley a big wink. "That's it! I'm off
to college!"

"But I'll miss you!"

"I'll come home for visits. You know
I'm leaving you in charge while I'm away.
Don't let me down."

"Who will
read me
stories?"

The next Saturday morning, the corners of Ashley's mouth drooped when she looked into Mark's empty room. He had been gone for five days, but it seemed like forever. When she slowly plodded down the stairs and into the kitchen, Mom and Dad were talking.

"Maybe we should take Oliver to the vet," Mom said. Mark's big, beautiful dog, Oliver, was on the floor staring at the kitchen door. "He won't eat. He just lies there waiting for Mark."

Dad smiled at Ashley and gave her a hug. Mom poured cereal and milk into a bowl for her.

"You can help us in the garden after you eat, Ashley," said Mom. "We all miss Mark. If we stay busy, we won't think about it so much."

Ashley plopped down next to Oliver as Mom and Dad went outside. The big brown dog didn't move. His sad, hopeful eyes gazed at the door.

"I miss Mark, too," said Ashley, scratching his ears. Oliver looked at Ashley and whimpered.

"If you want, I'll be your new best friend. You can sleep on my bed. I won't mind at all."

Ashley jumped up. She got Oliver's bowl of food and set it in front of him with a clatter. Milk splashed on the floor as she carried her cereal bowl from the table. She settled next to Oliver.

Name _____ Date _____

"If you'll eat your breakfast, I'll eat mine," she said. She stuffed a spoonful of cereal in her mouth. Oliver slowly licked up the spilled milk. She put some of her cereal in Oliver's bowl. She smiled when he began munching his food.

Ashley put her arms around Oliver and felt much better. Being in charge was going to be a full-time job.

"If you'll eat your breakfast, I'll eat mine."

**Now answer Numbers 1 through 5. Base your answers on the
story "Missing Mark."**

1 Which of the following BEST describes how the author introduces
the story?

(A) Ashley is watching Mark pack.

(B) Mom and Dad are talking about Oliver.

(C) Ashley tells Oliver that she misses Mark.

(D) Mark tells Ashley that he is leaving her in charge.

2 What is the FIRST thing Ashley does on Saturday morning?

(F) She goes into the kitchen.

(G) She looks into Mark's room.

(H) She sits down next to Oliver.

(I) She gives Oliver some cereal.

3 Read this sentence from the story.

**When she slowly plodded down the stairs and into
the kitchen, Mom and Dad were talking.**

What does this sentence tell you about Ashley?

(A) She feels sad.

(B) She feels sick.

(C) She feels happy.

(D) She feels hungry.

4 Why does Mark leave home?

(F) to find a job

(G) to go to college

(H) to get a new dog

(I) to visit Grandma

5 Read the dictionary entry below.

spill, *verb* **1.** to shed. **2.** to scatter. **3.** to let the wind out of. **4.** to run from a container.

Read this sentence from the story.

Oliver slowly licked up the spilled milk.

Which meaning BEST fits the way the word *spilled* is used in the sentence above?

(A) meaning 1

(B) meaning 2

(C) meaning 3

(D) meaning 4

Name _____ Date _____

**Read the articles "A Star Is Born" and "Nelson the Great"
before answering Numbers 6 through 11.**

A Star Is Born

Mia Hamm was born in 1972. As a baby, she had problems
with one of her feet. Her mom and dad did not know if she would
ever walk or run or kick a ball, but she learned to do all of these
things. Mia's parents did not know that she would grow up to be a
big star, but she did. She became a soccer star!

Soccer is a game in which two teams play against each other.
Each team has eleven players. The players cannot move the
ball with their hands or arms. Each team tries to score points by
kicking the ball into the goal. The winner is the team that gets the
most points.

Mia started playing soccer when she was only five years old.
By the time she was fifteen, she was such a good player that she

started winning prizes. Mia loved playing the game, and people liked watching her. After she finished school, she continued to play. She played soccer games all over the world and helped her team win many games.

A lot of girls who watched Mia play wanted to be just like her. Mia wanted to show the girls how to have a dream and work for it, so she started teaching them how to play soccer. Now many girls love playing soccer as much as Mia does.

Nelson the Great

John Byron Nelson was born February 4, 1912, near Waxahachie, Texas. His name was John, but he was always called Byron. When he was just eleven years old, he became very sick. He came down with typhoid fever. With typhoid fever, the body reacts with a fever and stomach pains. Byron lost about half of his body weight when he was sick. He got better though. And Byron went on to be a very important golfer.

A caddy might carry a golfer's bag or pull a cart like this.

When Byron was about twelve, he worked as a caddy. He worked hard to carry things for golfers on the golf course. But the golf course didn't let caddies play golf. That didn't stop Byron. He would play in the dark. He would put his white handkerchief near the holes. That way he could find the holes in the night. At the age of fourteen, Byron played in a golf match just for caddies. It was his first win!

Byron went on to have many other wins in golf. He won the U.S. Open, the U.S. Masters, and the Western Open. He was given many awards for being such a great golfer. Byron set a very important record, too. In one year, he won 18 out of 30 golf matches!

Sadly, Byron Nelson died September 26, 2006. Nelson was not a dime a dozen. There's no golfer like Byron Nelson. He set a good example for golfers to follow.

Now answer Numbers 6 through 11. Base your answers on the articles "A Star Is Born" and "Nelson the Great."

6 What is the article "A Star Is Born" MOSTLY about?

(F) how the game of soccer is played

(G) how Mia Hamm helped her team win

(H) how Mia Hamm became a soccer star

(I) why Mia Hamm teaches girls how to play soccer

7 In the article "A Star Is Born," which reason BEST explains why Mia began teaching girls to play soccer?

(A) People liked to watch Mia play soccer.

(B) Mia continued to play soccer after she finished school.

(C) Mia wanted to show the girls how to work for a dream.

(D) Mia began winning prizes because she was a good player.

8 In the article "Nelson the Great," what do the words under the picture tell you about golf caddies like Nelson?

(F) They have wheels.

(G) They pull a cart or carry clubs.

(H) The play golf at clubs with others.

(I) They contain bags, clubs, and balls.

Name _____ Date _____

9 Read this sentence from the article "Nelson the Great."

Nelson was not a dime a dozen.

What does the author mean by the phrase *not a dime a dozen* in the sentence above?

Ⓐ Nelson was common, just like a dime.

Ⓑ Nelson did not make money playing golf.

Ⓒ Nelson was memorable, or hard to match.

Ⓓ Nelson did not take money for his service.

10 In what way are Mia Hamm and Byron Nelson ALIKE?

Ⓕ They both became coaches.

Ⓖ They both overcame hard times.

Ⓗ They were born in the same year.

Ⓘ They were both good soccer players.

11 Why did the authors MOST LIKELY write these articles?

Ⓐ to share their opinions on sports

Ⓑ to tell funny stories about sports

Ⓒ to convince you to start playing sports

Ⓓ to inform you about important sports players

Read the story "How We Dare to Share" before answering Numbers 12 through 15.

How We Dare to Share

Do you have to share with someone at your house? I think everyone does. I know I have to share with my brother all the time. This is something we used to fight about almost every day. My brother would say that I got the bigger piece of pie. I would say that he got the bigger piece of cake.

Our parents did not like all of this fighting. One night our family was having some ice cream. My brother said that I had more. I said that he had more. I wanted to get a measuring cup to measure. My mother frowned. She made us put the ice cream back in the freezer until the next day.

Our mother and dad said that we had to find a way to solve this problem. My brother laughed and said that every time there was a larger piece of something, he should get it. I did not think that was funny at all.

I said that I was good at measuring. I could cut the pieces or get the servings and make sure they were the same size. My brother said we should take turns measuring and serving dessert. He said that would be fair.

Name _____ Date _____

Then I thought that we should take turns at something else, too. One person would get the servings. Then the other person would pick which serving he or she wanted. Now, if you are getting the servings and you know that you will get second choice, you will make sure to cut them fairly!

So now the only problem we have is remembering whose turn it is to serve and whose turn it is to pick first. I guess we will work on that problem next.

Now answer Numbers 12 through 15. Base your answers on the story "How We Dare to Share."

12 Why does the mother make the children put the ice cream back in the freezer?

- Ⓕ It is starting to melt.
- Ⓖ She wants to eat it later.
- Ⓗ The children are fighting.
- Ⓘ The children are not hungry.

13 Read this sentence from the story.

> **Now, if you are getting the servings and you know that you will get second choice, you will make sure to cut them fairly!**

What does the word *fairly* mean in the sentence above?

- Ⓐ not fair
- Ⓑ in a fair way
- Ⓒ used to be fair
- Ⓓ without being fair

14 What do the children do AFTER the parents tell them to find a way to solve their problem?

- ⓕ They think of a plan.
- ⓖ They laugh at each other.
- ⓗ They eat more ice cream.
- ⓘ They pout and leave the room.

15 Read this sentence from the story.

My brother laughed and said that every time there was a larger piece of something, he should get it.

What does this sentence tell you about the brother?

- ⓐ He is proud of his sister.
- ⓑ He is afraid of his sister.
- ⓒ He likes to tease his sister.
- ⓓ He wants to help his sister.

Read the story "Ben Franklin and His First Kite" before answering Numbers 16 through 20.

Ben Franklin and His First Kite

written by Stephen Krensky

illustrated by Bert Dodson

Ten-year-old Benjamin Franklin was hard at work in his father's candle shop. He was cutting wicks. He carefully laid out each one.

Ben stretched his arms and let out a yawn. Candles could be tall or short, fat or thin, and even different colors. But there was nothing fun about candles for Ben.

"When do you think we'll be done today?" Ben asked his father.

"Soon enough," his father answered. "Why? Do you have special plans?"

Ben's father smiled.

It was a rare day indeed when Ben did not have a plan in mind.

"Yes," said Ben. "I want to try an experiment at the millpond."

"You'll be swimming, then?" his father asked.

Ben grinned. "Partly," he said.

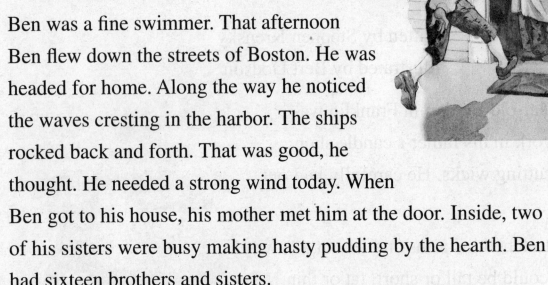

His father nodded. Ben was a fine swimmer. That afternoon Ben flew down the streets of Boston. He was headed for home. Along the way he noticed the waves cresting in the harbor. The ships rocked back and forth. That was good, he thought. He needed a strong wind today. When Ben got to his house, his mother met him at the door. Inside, two of his sisters were busy making hasty pudding by the hearth. Ben had sixteen brothers and sisters.

"Ben," his mother said, "why are you in such a hurry?"

Ben told her about his plan.

"Since your father approves, I won't keep you," said his mother. "Just be back for supper."

Ben nodded. He ran to get the kite he had made the week before. Then he left the house. At the millpond a few of Ben's friends had arrived to watch.

Name _____ Date _____

"You've picked a poor place to fly a kite," said one.

Ben shrugged. "I'm doing an experiment," he said.

Ben got undressed. He gave his clothes to one of his friends.

"Please carry these to the other side of the pond," he said.

"What are you going to do?" asked the other boys. "Carry the kite while you swim?"

"No," said Ben. "The kite is going to carry me."

"But that kite's nothing special. It's just paper, sticks, and strings," said one boy.

"That's true," Ben said. "But you see, the kite isn't the invention. The invention is what I'm going to do with it."

Ben raised the kite in the air. Once the wind had caught and carried it aloft, Ben walked into the water. There he lay on his back, floating.

"I'm going to cross this pond without swimming a stroke," said Ben.

The wind tugged on the kite. The kite string tightened. The water began to ripple at Ben's feet. The kite was pulling him!

The boys whooped and hollered as Ben glided across the pond. Finally he reached the other side. The other boys met him there.

"That was amazing!" said one.

"You crossed the whole pond without swimming a stroke," said another.

"What will you do next?" they asked.

"Another invention?"

"A different experiment?"

Ben didn't know. But he was sure he would think of something.

Name _____ Date _____

Now answer Numbers 16 through 20. Base your answers on the story "Ben Franklin and His First Kite."

16 Why does Ben want to be finished working with his father?

    Ⓕ   He is sleepy.

    Ⓖ   He is hungry.

    Ⓗ   He has plans for an experiment.

    Ⓘ   He wants to play with his friends.

17 Read this sentence from the story.

> **Inside, two of his sisters were busy making hasty pudding by the hearth.**

Which word has the SAME root as the word *busy* in the sentence above?

    Ⓐ   bus

    Ⓑ   buy

    Ⓒ   busted

    Ⓓ   business

18 What happens AFTER Ben gets his kite to fly?

    Ⓕ   Ben plans his experiment.

    Ⓖ   The kite falls into the water.

    Ⓗ   Ben takes the kite to the pond.

    Ⓘ   The kite pulls him across the pond.

19 Read this sentence from the story.

"I'm doing an experiment," he said.

Which two guide words would MOST LIKELY be at the top of a dictionary page that has the word *experiment*?

Ⓐ event • everybody

Ⓑ exact • example

Ⓒ expect • express

Ⓓ extra • eye

20 Which sentence BEST describes Ben?

Ⓕ He likes to try new things.

Ⓖ He likes making people laugh.

Ⓗ He wants to spend more time with his family.

Ⓘ He wants to make candles when he grows up.

Name _____ Date _____

Phonics

Answer Numbers 21 through 30. Choose the best answer for each question.

㉑ Which word has the SAME vowel sound as the word *cute* in the sentence below?

Fuzz is my cute little pet hamster.

- Ⓐ coat
- Ⓑ dust
- Ⓒ shake
- Ⓓ used

㉒ Which word has the SAME sound as the underlined part of the word *tail* in the sentence below?

Fuzz looks like a big brown mouse without a t<u>ai</u>l.

- Ⓕ loaf
- Ⓖ played
- Ⓗ straw
- Ⓘ team

23 Which word has the SAME sound as the underlined part of the word *catch* in the sentence below?

If Fuzz gets away from me, he is very hard to cat<u>ch</u>.

(A) bath

(B) rich

(C) shack

(D) wash

24 Which word has the SAME vowel sound as the word *rude* in the sentence below?

He plays at night and keeps me awake, so I
might change his name to Fuzz the Rude!

(F) crust

(G) opened

(H) rules

(I) supper

25 Which word has the SAME sound as the underlined part of the word *cage* in the sentence below?

I make sure that Fuzz has everything he needs in his <u>c</u>age.

(A) chair

(B) king

(C) rice

(D) safe

Name _____ Date _____

26 Which word has the SAME sound as the underlined part of the word *show* in the sentence below?

I fill up his water bottle and sh<u>ow</u> him where the water comes out.

- (F) bond
- (G) float
- (H) lock
- (I) house

27 Which word has the SAME sound as the underlined part of the word *scrub* in the sentence below?

When his cage gets dirty, I <u>scr</u>ub it and line it with clean paper.

- (A) school
- (B) scrape
- (C) shrub
- (D) skate

28 Which word has the SAME sound as the underlined part of the word *sleep* in the sentence below?

Fuzz likes to sl<u>ee</u>p in a little toy house.

- (F) better
- (G) meat
- (H) sled
- (I) well

87

29 What does *doesn't* mean in the sentence below?

I hope Fuzz doesn't get lonely when I'm not at home.

Ⓐ did not

Ⓑ do not

Ⓒ does not

Ⓓ doing not

30 Which word has the SAME sound as the underlined part of the word *maybe* in the sentence below?

M<u>ay</u>be I will get another hamster so Fuzz can have a friend!

Ⓕ lasting

Ⓖ marked

Ⓗ meantime

Ⓘ trades

Revising and Editing

Read the introduction and the story "Making Model Airplanes" before answering Numbers 1 through 5.

Victor wrote this story about his favorite hobby. Read his story and think about the changes he should make.

Making Model Airplanes

(1) I love making model airplanes. (2) One reason is that I learn about the past. (3) War airplanes are my favorite models. (4) To build. (5) When I build these airplanes, I read about the wars in which they were used.

(6) I also like building airplanes because it takes skill. (7) First, I work out how the pieces go together. (8) Next, I glue the pieces in place. (9) Lastly, I paints all the details to match the real airplane. (10) I feel proud of my work when I do a good job.

(11) The best thing about building airplanes is doing it with my dad. (12) We make a great temm. (13) He teach me about all of

the models. (14) We have fun choosing which ones to make.
(15) We also spend hours together building the airplanes.

   (16) I hope you get to build a model airplane sometime. (17) It
is a lot of fun!

_____

**Now answer Numbers 1 through 5. Base your answers on the
changes Victor should make.**

① Look at sentence 2 again.

   (2) One reason is that I learn about the past.

Which sentence could BEST follow and support sentence 2?

   Ⓐ I read books about all the old airplanes that I build.

   Ⓑ I have learned to be patient and hold my hands steady.

   Ⓒ My dad has been making models since he was my age.

② Look at sentence 9 again.

   (9) Lastly, I paints all the details to match the real airplane.

How should this sentence be changed?

   Ⓕ change *paints* to **paint**

   Ⓖ change *match* to **matches**

   Ⓗ change the period (.) to a question mark (?)

Name _____ Date _____

❸ Look at sentence 12 again.

(12) We make a great temm.

How should this sentence be changed?

(A) change *We* to **we**

(B) change *make* to **makes**

(C) change *temm* to **team**

❹ Look at sentence 13 again.

(13) He teach me about all of the models.

How should this sentence be changed?

(F) change *He* to **he**

(G) change *teach* to **teaches**

(H) change *models* to **model**

❺ Look at these sentences again.

(3) War airplanes are my favorite models.

(4) To build.

(17) It is a lot of fun!

Which sentence is NOT a complete sentence?

(A) sentence 3

(B) sentence 4

(C) sentence 17

Read the introduction and the article "Our Backyard Circus" before answering Numbers 6 through 10.

Shelly wrote this story about a show she put on with her friends. Read her story and think about the changes she should make.

Our Backyard Circus

(1) Last summer my friends and I put on a circus. (2) First, we made clown suits out of old clothes. (3) Next, we made a list of jokes and tricks. (4) We worked on our acts.

(5) When the circus was ready, our families came to watch the show. (6) I told jokes. (7) One friend stood on her head. (8) Another one walked on his hands. (9) Everyone was amazed when my dog Buster jumps through a hoop.

(10) The next act made everyone laugh. (11) We wore our clown suits and rode around on tricycles. (12) I honked a silly horn, and everyone laughed. (13) Can you guess what we did next. (14) We danced and sang funny songs. (15) At the end of the show, we all bumped into each other and fell down. (16) I think that was the moost fun of all. (17) Next year, I hope our circus will be better. (18) We will have just as much fun!

Now answer Numbers 6 through 10. Base your answers on the changes Shelly should make.

6 Look at these sentences again.

(2) First, we made clown suits out of old clothes.

(3) Next, we made a list of jokes and tricks.

(4) We worked on our acts.

What word should be added at the beginning of sentence 4?

Ⓕ Before,

Ⓖ Finally,

Ⓗ Tomorrow,

7 Look at sentence 9 again.

(9) Everyone was amazed when my dog Buster jumps through a hoop.

How should this sentence be changed?

Ⓐ change *dog* to **Dog**

Ⓑ change *jumps* to **jumped**

Ⓒ change the period (.) to a question mark (?)

Name _____ Date _____

8 Look at sentence 13 again.

  (13) Can you guess what we did next.

How should this sentence be changed?

Ⓕ change *Can* to **can**

Ⓖ change *guess* to **guessing**

Ⓗ change the period (**.**) to a question mark (**?**)

9 Look at sentence 16 again.

  (16) I think that was the moost fun of all.

How should this sentence be changed?

Ⓐ change *I* to **I'm**

Ⓑ change *think* to **thinks**

Ⓒ change *moost* to **most**

10 Look at these sentences again.

  (17) Next year, I hope our circus will be better.

  (18) We will have just as much fun!

How can these sentences BEST be combined?

Ⓕ Next year, I hope that our circus will be better we will have just as much fun!

Ⓖ Next year, I hope that our circus will be better. we will have just as much fun!

Ⓗ Next year, I hope that our circus will be better, and we will have just as much fun!

Writing Opinions

Read the prompt and plan your response.

> Most people have a special place they would like to visit with others.
>
> Think about a special place you would like to visit with your class on a trip.
>
> Now write to persuade your teacher to take your class on a trip to that special place.

Use this space to make your notes before you begin writing. The writing on this page will NOT be scored.

_____

_____

_____

_____

_____

Name _____ Date _____

Begin writing your response here. The writing on this page and the next page WILL be scored.

_____

_____

_____

_____

_____

_____

_____

_____

_____

_____

Name _____ Date _____

_____

_____

_____

_____

_____

_____

_____

_____

_____

_____

Name _____ Date _____

Reading Complex Text

Read the story "A Reason to Dance Once More." As you read, stop and answer each question. Use evidence from the story to support your answers.

A Reason to Dance Once More
A Cherokee Legend

Long ago, when the earth was young, a butterfly lost her best friend while he was far away from home. She was so upset, she removed her beautiful, many-colored wings. Then she wrapped herself in a gray cocoon. "I fear that I will never be happy again. The world has lost its joy and its color," the butterfly said. She would not eat and she could not sleep. Friends tried to help her. Nothing could be done. She would not show feelings of happiness.

1 How does the butterfly feel about her best friend?

_____

_____

_____

Since nothing could make her happy, the butterfly packed up her wings and went on a long journey. "I will leave this place and try to leave my sadness behind," she said. But the sadness never left her. She traveled far and wide. She traveled to high mountains and low valleys. She passed through bright deserts and dark forests. She passed through all the hot, cold, wet, and dry places on the earth. In time, she had gone all over the world.

2 Why does the butterfly leave her home?

_____

_____

_____

On her travels, the butterfly refused to look up. She kept her
eyes down. She never once looked at the sky. She never looked at
the horizon. "I will always look down. I have no need to look at
the world in sadness. I will only look down at the colorless stones
on the ground," she said. Keeping her eyes down, she would step
on each stone she came across in every field, forest, creek, and
stream. Suddenly, she discovered one glimmering stone. It was
beautiful and colorful. Happiness filled her heart. Her sadness
disappeared like mist in the wind.

3 How does the glimmering stone make the butterfly feel?

_____

_____

_____

The butterfly threw away her gray cocoon. She took out her
beautifully colorful wings and put them back on. Happy once
again, she began to dance around. "I give thanks for another
chance to be happy in life. Color and beauty have returned," said
the butterfly. She returned to her home and told everyone how her
long journey healed her. They were all overjoyed to see the beauty
and color of her wings once again.

To this day, the Butterfly Dance shows an appreciation for nature. It gives thanks for the life and beauty of all living things.

4 What are TWO ways the butterfly shows she is happy once again?

_____

_____

_____

_____

Reading and Analyzing Text

Read the story "Go, Rosie, Go!" before answering Numbers 1 through 10.

Go, Rosie, Go!

It was another day to jump rope in gym class. Lynn and Mike turned the long rope in big, slow circles. The whole class hurried to get in line to wait for their turn to jump. Rosie stood at the back of the line and frowned.

Nick went first. He watched the rope and ran in at just the right time. Everyone counted. He made it all the way to 30 jumps. One after another, the kids watched the rope, ran in, and jumped. Then it was Rosie's turn. She watched the rope go around and around, but she didn't move. She felt like everyone was staring at her.

Rosie's friends cheered. "Go, Rosie, go!"

Rosie's cheeks turned red. At last, she gave it a try, but she failed. She tripped on the rope and fell to the ground. Rosie tried to hide the tears in her eyes.

Nick helped her up. "You just need some practice," he said in a kind way.

The truth was that Rosie had been jumping rope at home every day. With a short rope, she could jump 100 times without missing. She just couldn't figure out how to run in and start jumping with a long rope. Since she was the only kid on her street, there was no one to help turn the long rope.

103

Just then, Ms. Miles, the gym teacher, brought out a bunch of short jump ropes.

"Let's see how long each one of you can jump without missing," she said as she gave each student a short rope. "Ready, set, GO!"

Rosie smiled for the first time ever in gym class. As she jumped, she sang rhymes quietly to herself. Rosie tuned out the sound of all the other ropes and sneakers thumping on the ground.

After a while, Rosie realized that everyone was chanting. "Go, Rosie, go!"

She was the only one still jumping rope! The surprise almost made her miss a step, but she kept going. When at last she was too tired to go on, she stopped. The whole class cheered. Everyone was looking at her and smiling. Rosie smiled back!

Now answer Numbers 1 through 10. Base your answers on the story "Go, Rosie, Go!"

1 What is Rosie's problem at the beginning of the story?

   Ⓐ   She turns red because Nick makes fun of her.

   Ⓑ   She does not have any friends in her gym class.

   Ⓒ   She does not know the cheers that the other kids know.

   Ⓓ   She does not know how to start jumping with a long rope.

2 Read this sentence from the story.

    The whole class hurried to get in line to wait for their turn to jump.

What does the word *hurried* mean in the sentence above?

   Ⓕ   pushed

   Ⓖ   rushed

   Ⓗ   tried

   Ⓘ   waited

3 Read this sentence from the story.

    Rosie stood at the back of the line and frowned.

Which word means the OPPOSITE of the word *frowned*?

   Ⓐ   cried

   Ⓑ   hid

   Ⓒ   sat

   Ⓓ   smiled

Name _____ Date _____

4 Read this sentence from the story.

   She felt like everyone was staring at her.

What does the word *staring* mean in the sentence above?

- (F) laughing
- (G) looking
- (H) pointing
- (I) yelling

5 Read this sentence from the story.

   At last, she gave it a try, but she failed.

What does the word *failed* mean in the sentence above?

- (A) was not able to
- (B) did not want to
- (C) changed her mind
- (D) was not allowed to

6 What happens AFTER Rosie trips and falls?

- (F) Gym class begins.
- (G) Nick helps Rosie get back up.
- (H) Everyone lines up for a turn to jump.
- (I) Rosie practices jumping rope at home.

Name _____ Date _____

7 Read this sentence from the story.

"You just need some practice," he said in a kind way.

What does the word *kind* mean in the sentence above?

(A) nice or helpful

(B) one type or group

(C) alike in some way

(D) sort of or a little bit

8 Why does Rosie smile in gym class?

(F) She does something well at last.

(G) She knows the class will chant for her.

(H) She thinks that she is going to make a friend.

(I) She has planned a surprise for her classmates.

9 Read the chart below.

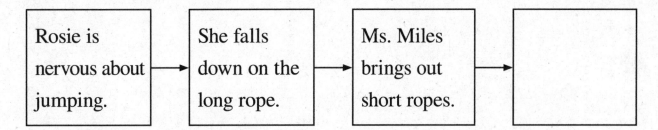

| Rosie is nervous about jumping. | → | She falls down on the long rope. | → | Ms. Miles brings out short ropes. | → | |

Which sentence BEST completes the chart?

(A) The class decides to play kickball.

(B) Nick wins the rope-jumping contest.

(C) Rosie is the last one still jumping rope.

(D) Rosie tries to hide in the back of the line.

Name _____ Date _____

10 How does Rosie feel when everyone looks at her AFTER she stops jumping with the short rope?

- Ⓕ foolish
- Ⓖ hurt
- Ⓗ mad
- Ⓘ proud

Read the article "Wildlife Hero" before answering Numbers 11 through 20.

Wildlife Hero

Animals in Trouble

Who will rescue a flying squirrel caught in a mousetrap? Who will help a snowy owl tangled in fishing line? Who will give a safe home to a bobcat with no claws? Mona Rutger—that's who! She has cared for thousands of injured animals. Mona runs a wildlife center in Castalia, Ohio, called Back to the Wild.

Mona's Story

Mona grew up on a farm. She spent a lot of time exploring the creeks and woods near the farm. She began learning about the local wildlife, too. Watching insects and animals filled her with wonder. She wanted to learn all about them.

As she got older, Mona did learn more about animals. She decided that she wanted to help animals. She used some of her family's land to start a wildlife center. It was a place where hurt animals could live until they were ready to go back to the wild. Many people brought Mona wild animals in need of

Back to the Wild is home to a bald eagle that can't fly. The eagle flew into power lines and broke its shoulders.

help. Some were baby animals that had lost their mothers. Others were animals that had been hit by cars. A few of the animals had eaten harmful chemicals. Mona helped them all.

A Hero Gets a Hand

Mona took care of the animals seven days a week. She didn't complain about being overworked, though. She knew the animals depended on her. In time, volunteers began to help her. Some people helped care for the animals. Others put money in a fund for the center. The fund helped pay for animal feed and medical bills. One friend wrote and told a television station about Back to the Wild. The letter led to a special award. Mona was named the Hero of the Year! She received a $10,000 prize from the television station. Mona used the money to help more animals.

Today, Mona is still taking care of animals. She also visits schools to teach children about protecting wild places and animals. She hopes her audiences will become heroes for animals, too!

Now answer Numbers 11 through 20. Base your answers on the article "Wildlife Hero."

11 Read this sentence from the article.

She has cared for thousands of injured animals.

Which word means almost the SAME as the word *injured*?

Ⓐ fierce

Ⓑ hurt

Ⓒ lost

Ⓓ pet

12 What was Mona like as a child?

Ⓕ curious

Ⓖ fearful

Ⓗ injured

Ⓘ quiet

13 Read this sentence from the article.

A few of the animals had eaten harmful chemicals.

What does the word *harmful* mean in the sentence above?

Ⓐ harm again

Ⓑ full of harm

Ⓒ one who harms

Ⓓ without any harm

Name _____ Date _____

14 How does Mona change AFTER she opens the wildlife center?

- Ⓕ She no longer enjoys learning about animals.

- Ⓖ She starts spending every day caring for animals.

- Ⓗ She stops teaching children about protecting wild animals.

- Ⓘ She starts asking people to adopt wild animals as pets.

15 Read this sentence from the article.

She didn't complain about being overworked, though.

What does the word *overworked* mean in the sentence above?

- Ⓐ not worked

- Ⓑ able to work

- Ⓒ worked again

- Ⓓ worked too hard

16 Read this sentence from the story.

She knew the animals depended on her.

What does the word *depended* mean in the sentence above?

- Ⓕ loved

- Ⓖ needed

- Ⓗ watched over

- Ⓘ were afraid of

112

Name _____ Date _____

17 Which word BEST describes Mona in the work place?

Ⓐ calm

Ⓑ dependable

Ⓒ slow

Ⓓ underworked

18 Read this sentence from the article.

She received a $10,000 prize from the television station.

What does the word *received* mean in the sentence above?

Ⓕ got something

Ⓖ gave something

Ⓗ grew something

Ⓘ guessed something

19 Read this sentence from the article.

Mona used the money to help more animals.

What can you tell about Mona from the sentence above?

Ⓐ She was generous to her cause.

Ⓑ She didn't appreciate the money.

Ⓒ She didn't think she deserved the money.

Ⓓ She cared more about animals than people.

113

Name _____ Date _____

20 Read this sentence from the article.

She hopes her audiences will become heroes for animals, too!

Why does the author MOST LIKELY use the word *heroes*?

Ⓐ to keep others from opening wildlife centers

Ⓑ to help others see they can make a difference like Mona

Ⓒ to prove that Mona made a lot of money helping animals

Ⓓ to show how popular you can become by taking care of animals

Name _____ Date _____

Phonics

Answer Numbers 21 through 30. Choose the best answer for each question.

21 Which word has the SAME sound as the underlined part of the word *farm* in the sentence below?

I spent last weekend at my grandparents' f<u>ar</u>m.

(A) around

(B) dark

(C) form

(D) grape

22 Which word has the SAME sound as the underlined part of the word *hard* in the sentence below?

I helped Grandpa because he had a lot of h<u>ar</u>d work to do.

(F) care

(G) horn

(H) start

(I) tray

23 Which word has the SAME sound as the underlined part of the
word *chores* in the sentence below?

While we were doing ch<u>ore</u>s, we felt a few raindrops.

(A) for

(B) frost

(C) roses

(D) those

24 Which word has the SAME sound as the underlined part of the
word *storm* in the sentence below?

Suddenly, the st<u>or</u>m hit and rain poured down.

(F) share

(G) shore

(H) stem

(I) stone

25 Which form of the word *run* is CORRECT and BEST completes the
sentence below?

We got soaked while we were _____ to the house.

(A) runing

(B) runnig

(C) running

(D) ruuning

Name _____ Date _____

26 Which word has the SAME sound as the underlined part of the word *dry* in the sentence below?

Grandma had some dr<u>y</u> towels waiting for us.

- (F) baby
- (G) clay
- (H) drink
- (I) sigh

27 Which form of the word *want* is CORRECT and BEST completes the sentence below?

She _____ us to stay inside and warm up for a while.

- (A) want
- (B) wantd
- (C) wanted
- (D) wantted

28 Which word has the SAME sound as the underlined part of the word *pie* in the sentence below?

We sat by the fire and had a piece of cherry p<u>ie</u>.

- (F) friend
- (G) fry
- (H) pail
- (I) pin

Name _____ Date _____

29 Which word has the SAME sound as the underlined part of the word *ready* in the sentence below?

I was read̲y to work again, so I looked out the window.

- Ⓐ dishes
- Ⓑ keeping
- Ⓒ kindest
- Ⓓ myself

30 Which word has the SAME sound as the underlined part of the word *pretty* in the sentence below?

The rain was gone, and a pretty̲ rainbow was in the sky!

- Ⓕ cried
- Ⓖ complete
- Ⓗ higher
- Ⓘ prizes

Revising and Editing

Read the introduction and the article "Barn Owls" before answering Numbers 1 through 5.

Luisa wrote this article about barn owls. Read her article and think about the changes she should make.

Barn Owls

(1) Barn owls is light brown birds with white faces. (2) There faces are shaped like a heart. (3) They are called barn owls because they like to live in old barns.

(4) Barn owls hunt at nite. (5) They eat mice and rats. (6) Soft feathers on their wings help them fly without making noise. (7) That helps them sneak up on the animals they hunt for food. (8) Barn owls feed themself by catching prey with strong claws and hooked beaks. (9) A bear has sharp claws because it is a hunter, too.

(10) Farmers like it when barn owls live on their farms. (11) The owls hunt the mice that eat the farmers' crops. (12) Some farmers will put wooden boxes in trees for the owls. (13) Barn owls makes their homes in these boxes.

Now answer Numbers 1 through 5. Base your answers on the changes Luisa should make.

1 Look at sentence 1 again.

(1) Barn owls is light brown birds with white faces.

How should this sentence be changed?

Ⓐ change *is* to **are**

Ⓑ change *light* to **lite**

Ⓒ change *faces* to **facs**

2 Look at sentence 13 again.

(13) Barn owls makes their homes in these boxes.

How should this sentence be changed?

Ⓕ change *makes* to **make**

Ⓖ change *their* to **there**

Ⓗ change *boxes* to **boxs**

3 Look at sentence 4 again.

(4) Barn owls hunt at nite.

How should this sentence be changed?

Ⓐ add a comma (,) after **owls**

Ⓑ change *hunt* to **hunts**

Ⓒ change *nite* to **night**

4 Look at sentence 8 again.

(8) Barn owls feed themself by catching prey with strong claws and hooked beaks.

How should this sentence be changed?

Ⓕ change *themself* to **themselves**

Ⓖ change *by* to **buy**

Ⓗ change *and* to **but**

5 Look at these sentences again.

(6) Soft feathers on their wings help them fly without making noise.

(9) A bear has sharp claws because it is a hunter, too.

(11) The owls hunt the mice that eat the farmers' crops.

Which sentence does NOT belong in this article?

Ⓐ sentence 6

Ⓑ sentence 9

Ⓒ sentence 11

Read the introduction and the story "My Dog Boomer" before answering Numbers 6 through 10.

Andy wrote this story about his favorite pet. Read his story and think about the changes he should make.

My Dog Boomer

(1) I've had some good pets, but Boomer is the best pet I've ever had. (2) He was a stray when we found him near my aunt's house in Tyler Texas. (3) Boomer was just a little puppi at the time.

(4) Now Boomer is almost as tall as I am when he stands on his hind legs. (5) He's a shaggy, white dog and has long ears.

(6) Boomer is funny. (7) When he sees a squirrel, he barks and turns in circles. (8) At the creek, he barks at dragonflies. (9) When they fly, he splashes around trying to catch them. (10) He hides whenever he sees someone wearing a hat, mittens or sunglasses.

(11) Boomer really loves myself. (12) He puts his paws on my shoulders and licks my face. (13) He and me sit together while I do homework. (14) At night, he sleeps next to my bed.
(15) Boomer is my best friend!

Name _____ Date _____

Now answer Numbers 6 through 10. Base your answers on the changes Andy should make.

6 Look at sentence 2 again.

(2) He was a stray when we found him near my aunt's house in Tyler Texas.

How should this sentence be changed?

Ⓕ add a comma (**,**) after *Tyler*

Ⓖ change *Texas* to **texas**

Ⓗ change the period (**.**) to a question mark (**?**)

7 Look at sentence 3 again.

(3) Boomer was just a little puppi at the time.

How should this sentence be changed?

Ⓐ change *was* to **were**

Ⓑ change *puppi* to **puppy**

Ⓒ change *time* to **tim**

Name _____ Date _____

8 Look at these sentences again.

(4) Now Boomer is almost as tall as I am when he stands on his hind legs. (5) He's a shaggy, white dog and has long ears.

Which sentence could BEST be added AFTER sentence 5?

Ⓕ   It has been two years since we found Boomer.

Ⓖ   His long, wavy hair makes him look a like a big mop.

Ⓗ   When Boomer gets scared, he hides behind Dad's chair.

9 Look at sentence 10 again.

(10) He hides whenever he sees someone wearing a hat, mittens or sunglasses.

How should this sentence be changed?

Ⓐ   Change *He* to **Him**

Ⓑ   Change *hides* to **hide**

Ⓒ   Add a comma (,) after **mittens**

10 Look at sentence 11 again.

(11) Boomer really loves myself.

How should this sentence be changed?

Ⓕ   add a comma (,) after Boomer

Ⓖ   change *loves* to **love**

Ⓗ   change *myself* to **me**

Writing to Narrate

Read the prompt and plan your response.

Most people have planned a nice surprise for someone.

Think about a nice surprise that a character could plan for someone.

Now write a story about a character who plans a nice surprise for someone.

Use this space to make your notes before you begin writing. The writing on this page will NOT be scored.

_____

_____

_____

_____

_____

_____

Name _____ Date _____

**Begin writing your response here. The writing on this page
and the next page WILL be scored.**

_____

_____

_____

_____

_____

_____

_____

_____

_____

_____

Name _____ Date _____

_____

_____

_____

_____

_____

_____

_____

_____

_____

_____

_____

Reading Complex Text

Read the article "From Eggs to Birds." As you read, stop and answer each question. Use evidence from the article to support your answers.

From Eggs to Birds

Birds, such as robins, hatch from eggs. Mother birds watch over their eggs to keep them safe. When their babies are born, mother birds take care of them until they can live on their own.

1 How do mother birds help their babies?

_____

_____

_____

Name _____ Date _____

Making Nests

Most birds make nests to keep their eggs safe. Birds collect things, such as twigs, to help build their nests. Birds use their beaks to connect the twigs together. They may also add grass or mud. The nest starts to look like a bowl. When the nest is done, the mother birds can lay their eggs.

2 What does the word *connect* mean in this article?

_____

_____

_____

Growing Inside Eggs

After a mother bird lays its eggs, it sits on them to keep them warm. This helps the baby bird grow inside the egg. Soon the baby starts to look like a tiny bird. Birds can chirp inside their eggs. Their parents can even hear them!

Hatching Eggs

Once a bird is strong enough, it will begin to hatch. Hatching starts from inside the egg. On its beak, the baby bird has a bump called an egg tooth. The bird pokes holes in its shell with its egg tooth. Finally the baby bird gets out of the shell.

Getting Strong

Baby birds are born with closed eyes and thin feathers. They aren't strong enough to leave the nest. Their mothers bring them food. This helps the birds get stronger. Thicker feathers grow on their bodies.

3 Under which heading can you find how the baby birds get out of their eggs?

_____

_____

_____

Growing Up

Birds learn how to take care of themselves by watching their parents. They learn to find food from their parents. They even sing the same songs they hear their parents sing. Once they have learned all they need, they move out of the nest.

Name _____ Date _____

4 What does the author want to describe in this article?

_____

_____

_____

_____

_____

Reading and Analyzing Text

Read the story "Soup and More Soup" before answering Numbers 1 through 5.

Soup and More Soup

"Grandma is coming for a visit," Dad said. "Let's make something special to eat."

"I know just what we should make," said Sophia. "Grandma gave us a recipe for her delicious white bean soup. Let's surprise her with that."

Marcos said that soup was his favorite, and Dad agreed that the bean soup was a great idea. Dad found the recipe and said, "We need to start with two cups of beans. That doesn't sound like very much. It must mean two cups for each person. If we want to make soup for four people, then how many cups of beans will we need?"

"Eight!" Sophia and Marcos shouted at the same time. They both loved to solve math problems.

Dad laughed. Then they figured out how many tomatoes, carrots, and cups of water they would need for four servings.

Dad, Sophia, and Marcos took turns adding the items to the soup pot.

Sophia said, "I think we're going to need a bigger pot!"

Dad found a bigger pot. "This is a lot of soup," he said.

Dad read the recipe again. At the bottom of the page, Grandma had written that the recipe made enough for four servings. Dad had not seen that the first time he read the recipe. He explained what had happened to Sophia and Marcos. "What is four times four?" he asked.

"Sixteen!" they both answered.

"So we have enough soup for sixteen people," Dad said.

Sophia knew just what to do. When Grandma rang the doorbell, all their neighbors were waiting in the backyard to visit with Grandma, too!

Name _____ Date _____

Now answer Numbers 1 through 5. Base your answers on the story "Soup and More Soup."

1 How do Marcos and Sophia feel about Grandma's visit?

(A) excited

(B) nervous

(C) sad

(D) sleepy

2 Read the dictionary entry below.

---

recipe, *noun* **1.** a style. **2.** a formula. **3.** a set of directions. **4.** a prescription for medicine.

Read this sentence from the story.

Grandma gave us a recipe for her delicious white bean soup.

Which meaning BEST fits the way the word *recipe* is used in the sentence above?

(F) meaning 1

(G) meaning 2

(H) meaning 3

(I) meaning 4

Name _____ Date _____

3 What is Marcos' favorite food?

Ⓐ beans

Ⓑ carrots

Ⓒ soup

Ⓓ tomatoes

4 How are Marcos and Sophia ALIKE?

Ⓕ Both are good at math.

Ⓖ Both are the same age.

Ⓗ Both visit Grandma often.

Ⓘ Both invite the neighbors.

5 Why does the family make so much soup?

Ⓐ They didn't see Grandma's note.

Ⓑ They wanted to save some for later.

Ⓒ They didn't like to solve math problems.

Ⓓ They planned on feeding their neighbors.

**Read the poem "The Potato's Path" before answering
Numbers 6 through 10.**

The Potato's Path

I love to eat potatoes.

Yum, yum, yum, yum, yum!

But when I eat potatoes,

I wonder where they're from.

Do they drop down from the air

Or wash in from the sea?

My brain keeps asking where,

So Mom sat down and told me.

"Potatoes come from far away,

From a farm out on the plain.

The farmer picks them every day

And puts them on a train.

Name _____   Date _____

They ride the train all day and night,

And when the sun comes up,

A team of workers use all their might

And load them on a truck.

The spuds are driven through the town

And to the grocer's door.

The grocer weighs them to the pound

And puts them in the store."

Potatoes make me happy!

I know just where they're from.

They've made a long, hard journey

To travel to our home.

Now answer Numbers 6 through 10. Base your answers on the poem "The Potato's Path."

6 Who is speaking in this poem?

- Ⓕ the grocer
- Ⓖ the farmer
- Ⓗ a person who likes potatoes
- Ⓘ a worker who loads potatoes

7 Which line from the poem tells what it is like to wonder where potatoes come from?

- Ⓐ "Yum, yum, yum, yum, yum!"
- Ⓑ "My brain keeps asking where,"
- Ⓒ "And when the sun comes up,"
- Ⓓ "The spuds are driven through the town"

8 Where do potatoes start their journey?

- Ⓕ at the store
- Ⓖ in a train
- Ⓗ on a farm
- Ⓘ on a truck

9 Read these lines from the poem.

> **The grocer weighs them to the pound**
> **And puts them in the store.**

What does the word *grocer* mean in the line above?

- Ⓐ someone who sells food
- Ⓑ someone who likes to shop
- Ⓒ someone who drives a truck
- Ⓓ someone who grows potatoes

10 Read this sentence from the poem.

> **Potatoes make me happy!**

Which word means the OPPOSITE of the word *happy* in the
sentence above?

- Ⓕ careful
- Ⓖ cheerful
- Ⓗ full
- Ⓘ sad

**Read the article "Who's Home in Prairie Dog Town"
before answering Numbers 11 through 15.**

Who's Home in Prairie
Dog Town?

by Catherine Ripley

It's a busy morning in prairie dog town.

"Grrr! Grrrr!" argue two black-tailed
prairie dog brothers, grinding their teeth.
Close by, Mom nibbles and cleans their
sister's short fur while a cousin dig, dig,
digs a hole. Farther away, Auntie snacks on
a blade of buffalo grass.

"Chirk, chirk!" warns Dad, who has spotted a golden eagle
high in the sky. All across town, prairie dogs watch the eagle and
chirk to alert others who have not seen it. When the eagle swoops
lower, Dad announces the danger loudly. "CHIRK!" In a flash,
the prairie dog families dive into their burrows. They wait safely
underground for the eagle to fly away.

Prairie dogs use their long, curved claws to dig lots of escape
holes, so they will always have safe spots to hide. They also dig
large, deep tunnels to live in. At the front door of their homes,
they mound up the earth. The small hill makes a great lookout
tower! Just inside the tunnel, there is usually a room where a

prairie dog can listen for danger but remain hidden. Deeper down is a nesting room for babies and maybe a sleeping room. All the homes have a back door. After all, some predators, such as black-footed ferrets, sneak into the tunnels to hunt prairie dogs. It's only smart to have more than one way out!

Prairie dog tunnels stay warm in the freezing winter and cool in the hot summer. They help improve the soil on the dry prairie, too. All that digging loosens the earth, allowing rain to seep in more deeply.

Prairie dogs don't just dig and dig. They eat and eat. Their nibbling keeps the tall grasses clipped short. Trimming the grass keeps it fresh and nutritious and makes room for other kinds of plants to grow. The variety of plants in prairie dog town attracts many different kinds of animals.

Each family of prairie dogs has its own burrow. There are lots of families in the town, which can cover miles of open prairie.

Antelope and bison often drop by to munch on the young, tender grass. Sometimes a bison will take a dust bath. It rolls around in the short grass and dirt to rub off the itchy pests on its back. The plants growing in prairie dog town also attract many insects, and the insects in turn attract the birds, mice, and lizards that eat them.

Yum, yum!

So, prairie dog town is home to lots of animals, not just prairie dogs. Rattlesnakes, burrowing owls, and rabbits even use abandoned prairie dog burrows for their homes.

Name _____ Date _____

Without all the nibbling and digging by prairie dogs, the prairie would be much less lively and healthy. And less noisy, too!

Mom pokes her head out of her front door. Has the eagle gone? Yes! Up she jumps. Leaning backward, she lets out a yip. "WEEE-OH!" Other heads poke out of burrows, and soon the two prairie dog brothers are back, arguing, tumbling, and playing across the prairie.

**Now answer Numbers 11 through 15. Base your answers on
the article "Who's Home in Prairie Dog Town?"**

11 What is this article MOSTLY about?

Ⓐ how prairie dogs find food

Ⓑ how prairie dogs form families

Ⓒ what happens inside a prairie dog town

Ⓓ what kinds of animals hunt prairie dogs

12 Read this sentence from the story.

They wait safely underground for the eagle to fly away.

What does the word *underground* mean in the sentence above?

Ⓕ to the ground

Ⓖ above the ground

Ⓗ beside the ground

Ⓘ beneath the ground

13 Why do prairie dogs build towers?

Ⓐ to stay warm

Ⓑ to spot trouble

Ⓒ to dig deep tunnels

Ⓓ to keep the grass short

Name _____ Date _____

14 What would a prairie dog MOST LIKELY do if an enemy crawled into its tunnel?

    (F)   take a dust bath

    (G) dig a bigger hole

    (H) run out the back door

    (I)   climb into the nesting room

15 Based on the pictures in the article, which BEST describes how prairie dogs eat?

    (A) lying down

    (B) standing up

    (C) in the water

    (D) with their hands

Name _____ Date _____

**Read the story "Zachary's Feather" before answering
Numbers 16 through 20.**

Zachary's Feather

by Catherine Ripley

illustrated by Helen Cogancherry

One day when Zachary was visiting his grandpa and grandma,
he found something on the grass.

"Look, Grandpa, a bird lost a pretty white feather," he said.

"Might be from a chicken," Grandpa said, "because it's so big.
Put it in your cap and you can be Yankee Doodle."

But Zachary wasn't listening. He was running back to the
kitchen.

"Grandma, Grandma," he called. "I need a glass of water!"

"Are you thirsty?" asked Grandma, getting a glass from the
cupboard.

Name _____ Date _____

Zachary dragged the kitchen stool over to the sink and climbed up. "I can do it," he said. He filled the glass with water.

"It's not for me," he told Grandma. He put the feather carefully into the glass of water and climbed down.

That night, after he had taken his bath and Grandma had read three stories to him, Zachary fell asleep. He dreamed that his feather sent down white tangled roots inside the glass, like the ivy his mother grew in water. From the top of the feather grew a beautiful feather vine, curling upward, branching out with soft downy tendrils, and stirring in the breeze from the open kitchen window.

In the morning, Zachary ran downstairs to see his feather vine. But the feather was sticking in the glass of water just as he left it.

After breakfast, Zachary took his feather outside and planted it in the flower garden.

That night he closed his eyes and dreamed of a tall, straight, feather tree, with many branches spreading out to shade the lawn, each branch covered with fluffy feather leaves, shining in the sunlight and swaying in the breeze.

After two days, the feather was still the same, only dirtier. Zachary washed and dried the feather. "I want to use my feather for something," he said fiercely.

"You could stick it in your baseball cap," Grandma said. Zachary shook his head. All morning, Zachary carried his feather around, thinking and thinking.

When he got up from his nap that afternoon, it was raining. "How would you like to paint some pictures?" Grandma asked, spreading newspapers over the kitchen table and getting some small jars of red, blue, and yellow paint.

"Oh, Grandma, oh, Grandma! Not a picture, no, not a picture!" Zachary exclaimed. "But I know how to use my feather!"

So Zachary sat at the table and, with some help from his grandma, he used his feather. He dipped it into the red paint and made a letter for his parents.

Dear Mommy and Daddy
I found a feather. It writes,
          Love, Zachary

Now answer Numbers 16 through 20. Base your answers on the story "Zachary's Feather."

16 Where does this story take place?

   Ⓕ in Zachary's dream

   Ⓖ at Zachary's school

   Ⓗ at Zachary's friends' house

   Ⓘ at Zachary's grandparents' house

17 At the beginning of the story, why does Zachary NOT listen to Grandpa?

   Ⓐ Zachary is too excited.

   Ⓑ Grandpa is being silly.

   Ⓒ Grandpa speaks too quietly.

   Ⓓ Zachary is busy writing a letter.

18 What happens in Zachary's FIRST dream?

   Ⓕ The feather becomes a tree.

   Ⓖ The feather becomes a vine.

   Ⓗ Zachary plants the feather in the garden.

   Ⓘ Zachary puts the feather in a glass of water.

19 Which sentence from the story BEST shows how Zachary feels when he finally thinks of what to do with the feather?

Ⓐ "Zachary shook his head."

Ⓑ "All morning, Zachary carried his feather around, thinking and thinking."

Ⓒ "'How would you like to paint some pictures?'"

Ⓓ "'Oh, Grandma, oh, Grandma!'"

20 Which pair of words from the story are most OPPOSITE in meaning?

Ⓕ bird, chicken

Ⓖ downy, soft

Ⓗ sunlight, shade

Ⓘ pretty, beautiful

Name _____ Date _____

Phonics

Answer Numbers 21 through 30. Choose the best answer for each question.

21 Which word is CORRECT and BEST completes the sentence below?

I like to daydream about life in the _____.

Ⓐ futer

Ⓑ future

Ⓒ futor

Ⓓ futhe

22 Which form of the word *help* is CORRECT and BEST completes the sentence below?

I'm sure there will be all kinds of _____ inventions.

Ⓕ helped

Ⓖ helpful

Ⓗ helping

Ⓘ helps

151

23 Which word has the SAME sound as the underlined part of the word *serve* in the sentence below?

   Robots may s<u>er</u>ve people their meals.

   Ⓐ bark

   Ⓑ deer

   Ⓒ hurt

   Ⓓ more

24 Which word has the SAME sound as the underlined part of the word *clean* in the sentence below?

   Machines might cl<u>ea</u>n a house at the flip of a switch.

   Ⓕ plan

   Ⓖ rake

   Ⓗ spend

   Ⓘ trees

25 Which word is CORRECT and BEST completes the sentence below?

   Maybe people will use their voices to _____ and open doors.

   Ⓐ mislock

   Ⓑ overlock

   Ⓒ prelock

   Ⓓ unlock

26 Which word has the SAME sound as the underlined part of the word *giant* in the sentence below?

Cars could even have giant wings to fly over traffic jams!

- Ⓕ gate
- Ⓖ jelly
- Ⓗ night
- Ⓘ sing

27 Which word is CORRECT and BEST completes the sentence below?

I _____ kids in the future will have a lot of fun.

- Ⓐ thick
- Ⓑ thin
- Ⓒ thing
- Ⓓ think

28 Which word has the SAME sound as the underlined part of the word *high* in the sentence below?

They might use jet shoes to run high in the sky!

- Ⓕ hay
- Ⓖ kite
- Ⓗ pig
- Ⓘ with

29 Which word has the SAME sound as the underlined part of the word *score* in the sentence below?

Jet shoes would make it easy to sc<u>ore</u> in basketball, too.

- (A) about
- (B) flower
- (C) scare
- (D) story

30 Which word has the SAME sound as the underlined part of the word *already* in the sentence below?

I wish we were in the future <u>a</u>lready!

- (F) crawl
- (G) pal
- (H) share
- (I) whale

154

Revising and Editing

Read the introduction and the article "What Your Brain Does" before answering Numbers 1 through 5.

Mia wrote an article about the brain. Read her article and think about the changes she should make.

What Your Brain Does

(1) The human brain has different parts. (2) A biggest part is used for thinking. (3) It help you read books, draw, and solve problems. (4) You also use it to remember things. (5) Without this part of your brain, you would froget everything!

(6) Another part of your brain is the boss of your muscles. (7) When your brain knows you want to run or swim, it starts giving orders. (8) It tells your arm and leg muscles to move. (9) Then it sends messages so your muscles will work together. (10) If your brain didn't do its job, all of the parts would not move at the right time.

(11) Another part of your brain are called the stem. (12) It is small, but it does a big job. (13) It tells your heart to beat! (14) It also makes sure that you breathe. (15) Your brain keeps working even when you sleep. (16) Its work is never done!

Now answer Numbers 1 through 5. Base your answers on the changes Mia should make.

1 Look at sentence 2 again.

> **(2) A biggest part is used for thinking.**

How should this sentence be changed?

Ⓐ change *A* to **The**

Ⓑ change *for* to **four**

Ⓒ change the period (**.**) to a question mark (**?**)

2 Look at sentence 3 again.

> **(3) It help you read books, draw, and solve problems.**

How should this sentence be changed?

Ⓕ change *help* to **helps**

Ⓖ change *read* to **reed**

Ⓗ change *problems* to **problem**

3 Look at sentence 5 again.

> **(5) Without this part of your brain, you would froget everything!**

How should this sentence be changed?

Ⓐ change *you* to **you've**

Ⓑ change *froget* to **forget**

Ⓒ change the exclamation mark (**!**) to a question mark (**?**)

4 Look at these sentences again.

> **(7) When your brain knows you want to run**
>
> **or swim, it starts giving orders.**
>
> **(8) It tells your arm and leg muscles to move.**
>
> **(9) Then it sends messages so your muscles will work together.**

What word should be added at the beginning of sentence 8?

Ⓕ Finally,

Ⓖ First,

Ⓗ Later,

5 Look at sentence 11 again.

> **(11) Another part of your brain are called the stem.**

How should this sentence be changed?

Ⓐ change *your* to **you're**

Ⓑ change *are* to **is**

Ⓒ change *called* to **calling**

Read the introduction and the story "Fun at the Lake" before answering Numbers 6 through 10.

Jason wrote this story about a trip to the lake. Read his story and think about the changes he should make.

Fun at the Lake

(1) My cousins and I went swimming. (2) My aunt set up a big umbrella with a stand. (3) She sat undr it and watched us from the shade.

(4) Suddenly, a big wind started blowing. (5) It lifted the umbrella up into the sky! (6) When the wind stopped, the umbrella landed upside down in a tree.

(7) My cousins and I ran to help. (8) First, we tried to reach the umbrella with long sticks. (9) The sticks we found weren't long enough. (10) We came up with a new plan. (11) We patted wet sand into small balls. (12) It was like a funny kind of basketball game!

(13) Each time a sand ball landed in the umbrella, it dropped a little. (14) Finally, it crashed to the ground. (15) My aunt sayed our idea was clever.

(16) My cousins and I wished the umbrella hadn't fallen down so soon. (17) It was fun playing sand basketball!

Now answer Numbers 6 through 10. Base your answers on the changes Jason should make.

6 Look at these sentences again.

   (1) My cousins and I went swimming.
   (2) My aunt set up a big umbrella with a stand.

Which sentence could BEST be added before sentence 1?

(F) I am the best swimmer in my family.

(G) Last summer I went to the lake with my cousins.

(H) On Saturdays, I have to do my chores before I can go outside.

7 Look at sentence 3 again.

   (3) She sat undr it and watched us from the shade.

How should this sentence be changed?

(A) change *She* to **I**

(B) change *undr* to **under**

(C) change *the* to **an**

8 Look at these sentences again.

> **(8) First, we tried to reach the umbrella with long sticks.**
>
> **(9) The sticks we found weren't long enough.**
>
> **(10) We came up with a new plan.**

Which word should be added at the beginning of sentence 10?

- (F) After
- (G) Then
- (H) While

9 Look at these sentences again.

> **(11) We patted wet sand into small balls.**
>
> **(12) It was like a funny kind of basketball game!**

Which sentence could BEST be added AFTER sentence 11?

- (A) We decided we would have a swimming race after lunch.
- (B) My cousins thought that digging in the sand was a lot of fun.
- (C) We threw the balls and tried to make them land in the umbrella.

Name _____ Date _____

10 Look at sentence 15 again.

(15) My aunt sayed our idea was clever.

How should this sentence be changed?

Ⓕ change *sayed* to **said**

Ⓖ change *was* to **were**

Ⓗ change the period (**.**) to a question mark (**?**)

Writing to Inform

Read the prompt and plan your response.

> Most people have some ideas about how to stay strong
> and healthy.
>
> Think about what you know about staying strong
> and healthy.
>
> Now write about how someone can stay strong and healthy.

Use this space to make your notes before you begin writing.
The writing on this page will NOT be scored.

_____

_____

_____

_____

_____

_____

_____

Begin writing your response here. The writing on this page and the next page WILL be scored.

_____

_____

_____

_____

_____

_____

_____

_____

_____

Name _____ Date _____

_____

_____

_____

_____

_____

_____

_____

_____

_____

_____

_____

Name _____ Date _____

Reading Complex Text

Read the articles "Places to See in NYC" and "Getting Around the Big City." As you read, stop and answer each question. Use evidence from the articles to support your answers.

Places to See in NYC

New York City is packed with famous places. There are so many places to go. It can be difficult to choose where to start. Here are a few must-see sites in this big city!

Coney Island

Coney Island is one of the best-known areas in New York City. People enjoy walking by the sandy beach. Visitors can find fun places to eat and shop. There are even rides, like roller coasters and bumper cars! You can learn about the ocean at the New York Aquarium. There you can see penguins, sea otters, and walruses.

Statue of Liberty

The Statue of Liberty is a national monument in New York City. Over one hundred years ago, the people of France gave the statue to the United States. The Statue is over 150 feet tall. You can visit it by riding a large boat called a ferry.

A French ship carried the pieces of the statue to the United States. The ship arrived in New York on June 17, 1885. Its cargo became Lady Liberty.

1 What is another name for the Statue of Liberty?

_____

_____

_____

Central Park

Central Park is a huge area in the middle of the city. It has lawns, trees, lakes, and streams. There is much to do here. You can exercise on the tennis courts, running track, or playgrounds. If you'd rather relax, then catch a puppet show at the Swedish Cottage.

Central Park is surrounded by buildings. It is one place people go to get *out* of the city—even though it's still *in* the city!

2 How does the picture of Central Park support the idea in the caption?

_____

_____

_____

Getting Around the Big City

People come from all over the world to eat at New York City's restaurants and hear its music. They also come to see the great museums and plays. It's no wonder that New York City is called "the city that never sleeps."

With so much going on, how do people get around? Many people in New York City ride the subway. A subway is a train that runs on electricity. It is one of the safest and cheapest ways to get around. If it's your first time riding the subway, these steps can help you.

1. Look at a map of the subway. Find where you are on the map. Then find where you need to go.

2. Check the times when the train arrives and departs. Weekend times can be different than the weekdays.

3. Make sure you have enough money for your ticket.

4. Once you have your ticket, make sure you get on the right train.

5. When you are ready to get on the train, let the arriving riders get off first. Then walk on and look for a seat. Don't be surprised if you have to stand!

Name _____ Date _____

3 What does the author want to explain in "Getting Around the Big City"?

_____

_____

_____

4 List one thing from each article that tells WHY New York City is a great place to visit.

_____

_____

_____

_____

_____

Reading and Analyzing Text

Read the stories "The Crow and the Pitcher" and "The Bird, the Watering Can, and the Stones" before answering Numbers 1 through 10.

The Crow and the Pitcher

Once there was a thirsty crow. He saw a pitcher of water. With much joy he flew to it, but he found there was only a little water left.

He tried to twist and turn to reach the water inside the pitcher. But he couldn't bend or reach far enough into it. With hopes of greater luck, he tried to turn the pitcher over. But he wasn't strong enough to knock the pitcher over.

He had one more thought. The sun shone bright and he noticed some glimmering pebbles lying nearby. He used his beak to pick them up. One by one, he put them in the pitcher. He watched the water rise. At last he was able to have a drink.

The Bird, the Watering Can, and the Stones

Rain had not fallen for many weeks. The creeks and ponds were all dried up. All morning, a little bird had been looking for water to satisfy her thirst.

Name _____ Date _____

At last she came across a watering can that a boy left near his garden. Inside the can, she noticed the long-lost water that she had been searching for.

"Ah, I must have that water!" she said. She reached her head in but could not get a drink. Her head would not fit into the hole on top of the watering can. She could see the water teasing her at the bottom of the can but could not reach it.

"I must have that water! I will have that water!" she cried. She grew thirstier and thirstier. Again, she stretched her head and moved it in many directions. She leaned in, but it still wouldn't fit.

"I know what I will do! I will use my beak to poke a hole into this watering can!" she said with hope. She tried and tried to poke the watering can. Instead of water, though, she only had a sore little beak.

The bird stopped. She seemed to be thinking very hard. She looked to her left. She looked to her right. She saw some stones lining a path near the garden.

"Stones, oh, stones! You can lend a hand!" she explained to the stones as if they could answer.

She picked up each stone and placed it in the can. She saw the water rise a bit so she kept dropping the stones. After much hard work, the water finally surfaced.

She put her beak into the water and drank. "What a nice refreshing drink after a day of hard work!" she said with delight.

Name _____ Date _____

Now answer Numbers 1 through 10. Base your answers on the stories "The Crow and the Pitcher" and "The Bird, the Watering Can, and the Stones."

1 Read this sentence from "The Crow and the Pitcher."

He saw a pitcher of water.

Which meaning BEST fits the way the word *pitcher* is used in the sentence above?

Ⓐ a kind of stone

Ⓑ a type of plant

Ⓒ a baseball player

Ⓓ a jug or container

2 Read this sentence from the story "The Crow and the Pitcher."

The sun shone bright and he noticed some glimmering pebbles lying nearby.

What does the word *glimmering* mean in the sentence above?

Ⓕ bouncing

Ⓖ hanging

Ⓗ hiding

Ⓘ sparkling

3 Read this sentence from the story "The Bird, the Watering Can, and the Stones."

> **Inside the can, she noticed the long-lost water
> that she had been searching for.**

Which word means almost the SAME as the word *noticed* in the sentence above?

Ⓐ feared

Ⓑ lost

Ⓒ saw

Ⓓ smelled

4 Read this sentence from the story "The Bird, the Watering Can, and the Stones."

> **She leaned in, but it still wouldn't fit.**

What does the word *leaned* mean in the sentence above?

Ⓕ bent

Ⓖ crashed

Ⓗ fell

Ⓘ grabbed

Name _____ Date _____

5 Read this sentence from the story "The Bird, the Watering Can, and the Stones."

> **"Stones, oh, stones! You can lend a hand!" she explained to the stones as if they could answer.**

What does the word *explained* mean in the sentence above?

- Ⓐ told
- Ⓑ pushed
- Ⓒ resulted
- Ⓓ tested

6 What is the MAIN reason the bird could NOT get to the water in the story "The Bird, the Watering Can, and the Stones"?

- Ⓕ Her beak was hurt so she couldn't use it.
- Ⓖ Her head wouldn't fit in the watering can.
- Ⓗ She couldn't find any stones to put in the watering can.
- Ⓘ She couldn't move her head in enough different directions.

7 How does the bird feel at the end of the story "The Bird, the Watering Can, and the Stones"?

- Ⓐ calm
- Ⓑ satisfied
- Ⓒ taller
- Ⓓ thirsty

Name _____ Date _____

8 How are the crow and the bird in the stories ALIKE?

   (F) Both are strong.

   (G) Both are thirsty.

   (H) Both find gardens and water.

   (I) Both give up on trying to get water.

9 How are the crow and the bird in the stories DIFFERENT?

   (A) The crow speaks, but the bird doesn't.

   (B) The crow gets water, but the bird doesn't.

   (C) The bird is very smart, but the crow isn't.

   (D) The bird tries to poke a hole to get water, but the crow doesn't.

10 What lesson can be learned from BOTH stories?

   (F) Don't be afraid to ask for help.

   (G) Sometimes you have to give up.

   (H) Working with friends always pays off.

   (I) If you don't reach your goal, keep trying.

**Read the article "Wonderful Water Creatures" before
answering Numbers 11 through 20.**

Wonderful Water Creatures

Many creatures live in the sea. Some live in warm water, and
others live in cold water. Some creatures live in deep seas, and
others live in shallow seas. What are some of these amazing
creatures, and where do they live?

Dolphins

Dolphins are creatures that live in the sea. Dolphins live in
warm and cold water. They have smooth, sleek bodies. This helps
them to swim very fast. Dolphins are mammals. That means
they need air to breathe. They breathe through
a blowhole. The blowhole is on top of their
heads. They swim up to get air and dive back
down to play. They are the most charming
creature of the seas!

Jellyfish

Jellyfish live in the sea, too. They look like
blobs that float in the water. Jellyfish don't have
any bones or brains, but they do have tentacles.
They can use their tentacles to catch fish. Some
jellyfish can even sting fish with their tentacles.

Some people, called divers, like to
explore the seas. With training, they
view sea creatures more closely. You
might say divers are the bravest sea
creatures of all!

Penguins

Penguins are birds that usually live in cold seas. An odd fact about penguins is that they are birds, but they can't fly! Penguins like to dive into water to find food, like fish and squid. They hop into the water, come up for air, and plunge right back in!

Sea Turtles

You'd most likely encounter a sea turtle in a warm sea. They have soft bodies that are covered with a hard shell. Their shells act as protective shields. Sea turtles have flippers to help propel them through the water. Many people think they swim peacefully and gracefully through the seas.

There are so many fascinating water creatures. Imagine what it might be like to see what's in the sea!

Name _____ Date _____

Now answer Numbers 11 through 20. Base your answers on the article "Wonderful Water Creatures."

11 Why did the author MOST LIKELY write this article?

ⓐ to convince you to become a diver

ⓑ to describe some animals in the sea

ⓒ to encourage you to visit the world's sea

ⓓ to share information about ocean temperatures

12 Which of these sentences is a FACT from the article?

Ⓕ "The blowhole is on top of their heads."

Ⓖ "They look like blobs that float in the water."

Ⓗ "You might say divers are the bravest sea creatures of all."

Ⓘ "Many people think they swim peacefully and gracefully through the seas."

13 Read this sentence from the story.

They have smooth, sleek bodies.

What word means the OPPOSITE of the word *smooth* in the sentence above?

ⓐ even

ⓑ flat

ⓒ rough

ⓓ soft

Name _____ Date _____

14 Which word is another name for *a group of animals that breathe air*?

(F) shield

(G) divers

(H) flippers

(I) mammals

15 Read this sentence from the article.

With training, they view sea creatures more closely.

What does the word *training* mean in the sentence above?

(A) good teaching

(B) correct clothing

(C) friendly support

(D) underwater cameras

16 Read this sentence from the story.

**An odd fact about penguins is that they
are birds, but they can't fly!**

What does the word *odd* mean in the sentence above?

(F) lucky

(G) sad

(H) untrue

(I) unusual

Name _____ Date _____

17 How are jellyfish DIFFERENT from penguins?

Ⓐ Jellyfish can fly.

Ⓑ Jellyfish catch fish.

Ⓒ Jellyfish have tentacles.

Ⓓ Jellyfish have bones and brains.

18 Read this sentence from the story.

**Sea turtles have flippers to help propel
them through the water.**

If *pro-* means "forward" and *-pel* means to "drive," what does
propel MOST LIKELY mean in the sentence above?

Ⓕ to stay still

Ⓖ to wear off

Ⓗ to sink down

Ⓘ to move forward

19 Which of these sentences is an OPINION from the article?

Ⓐ "Their shells act as protective shields."

Ⓑ "They are the most charming creature of the seas!"

Ⓒ "Dolphins are creatures that live in the sea."

Ⓓ "Some creatures live in deep seas, and others live in
shallow seas."

Name _____ Date _____

20 How are dolphins, jellyfish, penguins, and sea turtles ALIKE?

(F) None of them can fly.

(G) They all live in cold seas.

(H) They are all able to sting fish.

(I) None of them can breathe out of water.

Name _____ Date _____

Phonics

Answer Numbers 21 through 30. Choose the best answer for each question.

㉑ Which word has the SAME sound as the underlined part of the word *pool* in the sentence below?

Jim and Jan went swimming at the p<u>oo</u>l last week.

- Ⓐ bone
- Ⓑ hop
- Ⓒ mouth
- Ⓓ soup

㉒ Which word has the SAME sound as the underlined part of the word *new* in the sentence below?

Jan wore her n<u>ew</u> bathing suit.

- Ⓕ clue
- Ⓖ fly
- Ⓗ throw
- Ⓘ tree

23 Which word has the SAME sound as the underlined part of the word *looks* in the sentence below?

"The water lo̲o̲ks cold," she said.

- Ⓐ float
- Ⓑ gown
- Ⓒ noon
- Ⓓ stood

24 Which word has the SAME sound as the underlined part of the word *foot* in the sentence below?

Jim put his fo̲o̲t in the water.

- Ⓕ crew
- Ⓖ group
- Ⓗ put
- Ⓘ rope

25 Which word has the SAME sound as the underlined part of the word *frowned* in the sentence below?

He fro̲w̲ned and said, "Yes, it is chilly!"

- Ⓐ boat
- Ⓑ round
- Ⓒ saw
- Ⓓ soon

Name _____ Date _____

26 Which word has the SAME sound as the underlined part of the word *count* in the sentence below?

"Let's c<u>ou</u>nt to three and jump in," said Jan.

- Ⓕ ice
- Ⓖ on
- Ⓗ owl
- Ⓘ up

27 Which word has the SAME sound as the underlined part of the word *higher* in the sentence below?

"I can jump hi<u>gh</u>er than you!" laughed Jim.

- Ⓐ big
- Ⓑ nice
- Ⓒ train
- Ⓓ treat

28 Which word has the SAME sound as the underlined part of the word *spraying* in the sentence below?

Jim jumped in, spr<u>ay</u>ing water on Jan.

- Ⓕ cat
- Ⓖ might
- Ⓗ team
- Ⓘ wait

29 Which word has the SAME sound as the underlined part of the word *slowly* in the sentence below?

Jan got in the water sl<u>ow</u>ly.

- Ⓐ book
- Ⓑ lock
- Ⓒ soap
- Ⓓ through

30 Which word has the SAME sound as the underlined part of the word *really* in the sentence below?

The water was not r<u>ea</u>lly cold after all.

- Ⓕ bed
- Ⓖ crab
- Ⓗ mate
- Ⓘ meet

Name _____ Date _____

Revising and Editing

Read the introduction and the story "My Cat" before answering Numbers 1 through 5.

Kayla wrote this story about her cat. Read her story and think about the changes she should make.

My Cat

(1) I have a little cat named Meow. (2) I take care of her and fix her dinner every day. (3) My little brother wants to take care of her, but he isnt old enough. (4) He is only three years old. (5) I let him help me feed her sometime, and that makes him happy.

(6) I love playing with my cat. (7) Meows' favorite toy is a feather on a stick. (8) I shake it back and forth and she chases it. (9) She also has a little toy mose on a string. (10) I move it around, and Meow watches it quiet. (11) Then she jumps on it and bites it!

(12) When Meow gets tired, she likes to curl up on my bed. (13) Then I pet her soft fur and she goes to sleep purring.

Now answer Numbers 1 through 5. Base your answers on the changes Kayla should make.

1 Look at sentence 3 again.

> **(3) My little brother wants to take care of her, but he isnt old enough.**

How should this sentence be changed?

Ⓐ change *My* to **Mine**

Ⓑ change *isnt* to **isn't**

Ⓒ change *old* to **oldest**

2 Look at sentence 5 again.

> **(5) I let him help me feed her sometime, and that makes him happy.**

How should this sentence be changed?

Ⓕ change *let* to **letting**

Ⓖ change *her* to **she**

Ⓗ change *sometime* to **sometimes**

3 Look at sentence 7 again.

(7) Meows' favorite toy is a feather on a stick.

How should this sentence be changed?

Ⓐ change *Meows'* to **Meow's**

Ⓑ change *is* to **are**

Ⓒ change *on* to **to**

4 Look at sentence 9 again.

(9) She also has a little toy mose on a string.

How should this sentence be changed?

Ⓕ change *on* to **own**

Ⓖ change *toy* to **toi**

Ⓗ change *mose* to **mouse**

5 Look at sentence 10 again.

(10) I move it around, and Meow watches it quiet.

How should this sentence be changed?

Ⓐ change *I* to **Mine**

Ⓑ change *watches* to **watchs**

Ⓒ change *quiet* to **quietly**

Read the introduction and the article "A Lumpy, Bumpy Animal" before answering Numbers 6 through 10.

Marcus wrote this article about an animal he saw at the zoo. Read his article and think about the changes he should make.

A Lumpy, Bumpy Animal

(1) It looks like a pig with a bumpy face. (2) What is it? (3) It's a warthog!

(4) A baby warthog is very cute. (5) When it grows up, it gets bumps on its face and long hair on its back. (6) It isn't cute anymore! (7) It grows long, sharp tusks that help it fight off other animals. (8) It can run quickness on its long, thin legs.

(9) When it is hungry, itl'l eat berries and grass. (10) It gets doun on its knees. (11) Then it uses its snout to dig up roots and bugs.

(12) Female warthogs live together in a big group. (13) They help care for each others babies. (14) Each warthog mother knows her babies are very safe with the group.

Now answer Numbers 6 through 10. Base your answers on the changes Marcus should make.

6 Look at sentence 8 again.

(8) It can run quickness on its long, thin legs.

How should this sentence be changed?

- Ⓕ change *can* to **could**
- Ⓖ change *run* to **running**
- Ⓗ change *quickness* to **quickly**

7 Look at sentence 9 again.

(9) When it is hungry, itl'l eat berries and grass.

How should this sentence be changed?

- Ⓐ change *When* to **Why**
- Ⓑ change *itl'l* to **it'll**
- Ⓒ change *and* to a comma **(,)**

8 Look at sentence 10 again.

(10) It gets doun on its knees.

How should this sentence be changed?

- Ⓕ change *doun* to **down**
- Ⓖ change *its* to **it's**
- Ⓗ change *knees* to **news**

9 Look at sentence 13 again.

(13) **They help care for each others babies.**

How should this sentence be changed?

Ⓐ change *others* to **other's**

Ⓑ change *babies* to **baby's**

Ⓒ change *babies* to **babys'**

10 Look at sentence 14 again.

(14) **Each warthog mother knows her babies are very safe with the group.**

Which word BEST tells how safe the babies are?

Ⓕ each

Ⓖ knows

Ⓗ very

Name _____ Date _____

Writing Opinions

Read the story "Cricket and Cougar" before responding to the prompt.

Cricket and Cougar

One day a cougar was walking in the woods. He leaped on top of a log to take a look around. A tiny voice came from inside the log. "Hey, Cougar," said Cricket. "You are standing on the roof of my house. Please get off."

"You are in no place to tell me what to do," Cougar said firmly. He dropped his head. Cricket could feel Cougar's breath. "In this forest, I am the ruler of the animals!"

"Ruler or not," said Cricket fearlessly, "I have a cousin who is mightier than you."

"Impossible, little Cricket! No one is as mighty as I," Cougar said.

"Trust me or not. I know it's true that my cousin is mightier than you," Cricket said.

"Fine. Have it your way. Invite your cousin to prove what you say. I will meet him here tomorrow when the sun is high. If what you say is not true, then I will crush your log."

Cougar came the next day as promised. "Cricket! Cricket! Come out!" he shouted. "Where is your mighty cousin, poor little Cricket?"

Cricket stepped out from his log into the high sun. In the blink of an eye, tiny Mosquito zipped into Cougar's ear. Mosquito nipped and buzzed at Cougar's ear. Cougar pawed and pawed to force Mosquito away. Cougar's ear was red and itchy. The buzzing sound was causing his head to hurt.

"Stop! Stop, you tiny bug!"

But Mosquito didn't stop. He circled Cougar's ear many times over. Cricket hollered, "Now will you leave my log alone?"

Cougar had no choice but to agree. His ears were aching and itching, and he couldn't stand another second. With that, Mosquito came out and went into Cricket's log. And they never saw Cougar again.

Now respond to the prompt. Base your response on the story "Cricket and Cougar."

> In "Cricket and Cougar," Cricket gets his cousin to solve his problem for him.
>
> Think about whether or not this was the BEST way for Cricket to solve his problem.
>
> Write a response that tells why or why not.

Use this space to make your notes before you begin writing. The writing on this page will NOT be scored.

_____

_____

_____

_____

_____

_____

Name _____ Date _____

Begin writing your response here. The writing on this page and the next page WILL be scored.

_____

_____

_____

_____

_____

_____

_____

_____

_____

_____

Name _____ Date _____

_____

_____

_____

_____

_____

_____

_____

_____

_____

_____

Reading Complex Text

Read the stories "The Bee and the Firefly" and "The Lion and the Mouse." As you read, stop and answer each question. Use evidence from the stories to support your answers.

The Bee and the Firefly

by Erin Sanderson

It was a busy day in the forest. All of the insects flew around doing their work. Though none were as busy as Bee. Bee flew from flower to flower, taking only a minute here or there to rest.

Bee liked all of the insects except Firefly. Bee said, "Firefly shows off with the way she lights up at night. She thinks she is better than me."

The other insects did not agree. They thought that Bee was just jealous and wished he had Firefly's talent for making light.

---

❶ What does Bee think about Firefly? What do the other insects think about this?

_____

_____

_____

One day, Bee was very busy. Before he knew it, the sun had gone down and he was lost.

Firefly was flying by when she heard the worried buzzing of Bee. She flew over and found Bee, shivering and afraid.

"What's wrong, Bee?" the Firefly asked.

Bee said in a quiet voice, "I can't find my way back to my hive."

Firefly knew what Bee thought of her. She also knew that Bee needed help. "Do not worry. Follow my light. I will lead you back to your hive."

With that, Firefly lit up her light and led Bee back to his home.

Safe and sound, Bee turned to Firefly and said, "Thank you, Firefly. I was wrong about you. Please forgive me."

Firefly just smiled and flew away into the dark night.

2 How does Bee change in this story?

_____

_____

_____

The Lion and the Mouse

by Aesop

adapted by Michael Watrous

Lion lay asleep in the forest, her great head resting on her paws. Mouse came upon her unexpectedly. He squeaked in surprise. As he tried to run away, he ran across Lion's nose.

This woke Lion up. She was not happy. Her huge paw grabbed Mouse by his tail.

"Don't hurt me!" begged Mouse. "Please let me go and some day I will pay you back."

Lion laughed as she looked down at little Mouse. But she was feeling kind after her nap, so she let Mouse go.

❸ Why does Lion laugh at Mouse?

_____

_____

_____

A few days later, Lion was walking in the forest. Suddenly she heard a loud snapping sound and found herself trapped in a net.

She struggled to break free but could not. Tired and angry, she let out a loud roar.

Mouse heard Lion's voice and ran to her. He saw Lion trapped in the net. Quickly he began gnawing on the ropes of the net. Soon the ropes broke and Lion was free.

"Mouse, I laughed when you said you would pay me back," Lion said. "Now I see that even a mouse can help a lion."

❹ What are TWO ways Bee and Lion are ALIKE in these stories?

_____

_____

_____

_____

_____